THE ACADEMIC CRISIS
OF
THE COMMUNITY COLLEGE

SUNY Series,
Literacy, Culture, and Learning:
Theory and Practice

Alan C. Purves, Editor

THE ACADEMIC CRISIS
OF
THE COMMUNITY COLLEGE

Dennis McGrath
and
Martin B. Spear

STATE UNIVERSITY OF NEW YORK PRESS

Production by Ruth East
Marketing by Theresa A. Swierzowski

Published by
State University of New York Press, Albany

For information, address State University of New York
Press, State University Plaza, Albany, N.Y. 12246

Library of Congress Cataloging-in-Publication Data

McGrath, Dennis, 1946–
      The academic crisis of the community college / Dennis McGrath and
Martin B. Spear.
           p.   cm. — (SUNY series, literacy, culture, and learning)
      Includes bibliographical references.
      ISBN 0–7914–0562–1 (alk. paper). — ISBN 0–7914–0563–X (alk.
paper : pbk.)
      1. Community colleges—United States—Curricula.   2. Community
colleges—United States—Open admission.   3. Academic achievement.
I. Spear, Martin B., 1945–   . II. Title. III. Series.
LB2328.15.U6M39   1991
378.1'99—dc20   90–34599
                                                                          CIP

10 9 8 7 6 5 4 3 2 1

For
Charlene and Heather,
Egle and Kieran

CONTENTS

ACKNOWLEDGMENTS

Probably nothing would ever get written were it not for the assistance, encouragement, and support of relatives, friends, and colleagues. As this book has been long in the writing, our own have been patient practically beyond belief. We have tried out on them different approaches, new arguments, even figures of speech. What remains is what they couldn't talk us out of.

Richard Richardson and Steven Zwerling, critics of community colleges in their own right, encouraged us at the beginning of this project, and were kind enough to comment on an early draft. Obviously they may substantially disagree with us; nevertheless, without their support the book probably would not have progressed much further. Similarly, Alison Bernstein, then of the Ford Foundation, gave us the right push at the right time.

We warmly thank those people who read, and often reread, various chapters and graced us with their advice and suggestions: Jeffrey Berger, Huntley Collins, Elizabeth Dickey, Max Eirich, Judith Eaton, Ralph Faris, Gail James, Fred Pincus, Margot Soven, William Sullivan, Aram Terzian, and Elizabeth Warren. In particular, Evan Seymour and Charlene Leaver spent almost as much time with the manuscript as we did ourselves. Without these good people, both our thought and our expression would be clumsier still.

During the last decade we have benefitted from funding from both the Ford Foundation and the National Endowment for the Humanities. Much of our work traces back to the program experiments that funding allowed us to conduct. Besides that, the Ford grants enabled us to travel outside the walls of our college and our own region, to meet and interact with community college teachers and administrators from around the country, as well as legislators, researchers, and theoreticians. That experience has widened our perspective immensely, and we thank the Ford Foundation for giving it to us.

ix

We have been fortunate to have been asked to visit, speak, or consult at many colleges. Many of the ideas of this book saw first public expression in staff development activities and at in-service sessions at those host campuses. Always we tried to keep our learning curve steep, and our ears open. The colleges we visited, and the dedicated professionals we encountered, are owed a large debt of gratitude. Although too numerous to be named individually, they are remembered by us fondly.

An earlier draft of chapter one was presented at a meeting of the Transfer Alliance at UCLA. Chapter two was discussed at a summer workshop on transfer issues which included faculty from La Salle University, Temple University, and Community College of Philadelphia.

_____ Introduction

Because community colleges are so numerous and varied, they are only poorly captured in generalizations. Because they have evolved a distinctive academic culture, they are difficult to explain to "outsiders," or to people familiar only with traditional college life. Perhaps then it is well to begin, as is common with community college faculty, with the human experience—not exhaustively, to be sure, but as illustrative snapshots, "stories from the front."

It's the seventh week of the semester in a transfer-oriented program, one of the innumerable, innovative special programs that dot the landscape of community colleges. The professor, "teacher," sits in a seminar circle with thirteen students. Together they are discussing, or are meant to be discussing, an historical study on the development of prisons. Ten minutes into the session two more students arrive. Although they don't actually slam the door behind them as they enter, they allow it to slam, walk across the room and sit down outside the circle, scraping their desks as they move them, and fumbling with their coats and backpacks. Five minutes later another student enters; the whole process is repeated. During the next twenty minutes it is repeated three times more.

The entire class looks up and pauses as each student settles in, but the discussion then continues. The teacher follows his normal practice, with which students are by now long familiar. After a brief introduction, emphasizing the relation of the reading to previous materials, he raises a general question which is intended to initiate the conversation: what issue is the author raising and why does he take it to be significant? Three students raise their hands and offer, in turn, what they made of the reading. The teacher

1

looks around the circle at the many students who haven't spoken and notices that four of them don't have their books. He stops and asks why they've come to seminar without the book. Two students tell him that "we didn't buy it yet"; the other two guiltily look at their desks, while another student in the class laughs nervously. The teacher begins to get angry, saying that the book was assigned on the first day of the semester, and that they were reminded last week to read it. One of the offenders glares defiantly at him; the others lower their heads submissively. The teacher looks around the room saying that he is tired of all the lateness and that "if students don't have the book they shouldn't come to seminar." A young woman angrily erupts: "You can't say that to us. We paid our money for this course and we can get something even if we just listen." The teacher then shrugs his shoulders, throws up his hands, and tells the class to take a break.

Another teacher, another class. An ordinary college course, no frills, an "Introduction to Philosophy." There are many more students, about thirty or so, widely distributed in age, race, and ethnicity. The teacher is returning midterm examination papers; he is tentative and hesitant, with heavy heart, for the class has done poorly. He holds the papers while cautioning the class, and perhaps himself, against a too hasty despair. The students are sullen and suspicious while he explains to them what went wrong.

The examination had been of the take-home variety, a full week had been given for its completion. The question had seemed fair enough to the teacher. After they had read and discussed several important articles on the abortion controversy, students were pointedly asked how two of the articles related to each other. Not "what do you think about abortion" or "show how the controversy might be settled," but "show how the specific arguments and analyses relate." Almost nobody in the class had even made a pass at that question. Almost everybody was receiving a grade of "D."

As he returns the students' papers, the teacher thinks of, but says nothing about, the distance between their submissions and what he thinks of as a college-level paper. Despite the week's effort, most papers were less than a hundred words long. Most were handwritten, many illegibly. Most were simply ripped from a spiral notebook, the edges left ragged. One was very long, although very sloppily typed, marred further by the word "Phylosopy," displayed at the top center of the first page. One submission consisted entirely of a page xeroxed from a Bible, with a handwritten comment in the margin: "I agree with the word of god." Of the remainder most fell into one of two camps. Many students gave their "opinion" about abortion. Sometimes those students condemned the opposition to eternal torment; one paper assured the teacher that the writer would continue to pray for those who disagree with her. Of the students who did not use the examination as an opportunity to trumpet their beliefs, most took one of the articles and tried a quick summary of it. Occasionally, students summarized one article, then skipped a space on the page and summarized the other. Very frequently the names of authors were misspelled, sometimes more than one way on a single paper, even though the exam had been open book and take-home. Two students received grades of "F," having simply copied the editorial introductions to the articles from the anthology and handed that in. Only one of those is in class today; but he is visibly angry and hostile. He will follow the teacher back to his office protesting the injustice. After all, the student insists, since he agrees with the editor, who said it much better, why shouldn't he copy? But the more usual responses from the class hurt more. "Why isn't summarizing good enough," they ask, challenge really. And, "You asked for my opinion and I gave it," others say. "I have As and Bs in all my other classes" says the woman with the long typed paper for a Phylosopy course. One student, sensing the rise in the tension level, reassures the teacher that he ought not to take things personally. "I have only myself to blame," she says, "if I wasted my money on this course." The teacher is only human and the subtext from these people he cares so much about is not buried very deeply: "What's wrong with *you* anyway?" Even before the class period is over he has begun revising the course and rethinking requirements.

These tales are not intended to capture the full reality of community colleges. At any community college comfort can be found with little more than a glance—a mathematics class where students quietly work on problems while the teacher moves from one student to another, nursing students taking notes as a biology teacher lectures, a group of data processing students working together on a class project. On the other hand, the stories would not surprise many community college teachers. They respond to them with much sympathetic body language, smiles and nods of recognition, followed by vivid relating of similar experiences. Still, the stories are meant to be more than just two more horror stories of the sort that teachers everywhere love to share. Of course they are our stories: those were our classes; we were the teachers. And despite the details of time, and place, the idiosyncrasies of course content and pedagogical style, they do capture something about the routine experience of teaching and learning at community colleges. The need to make sense of those stories, and the many others that might be told, the stories of teaching and learning in the era of open access, has led us to write this book, to try to understand what community colleges have come to be, and what they might be.

Just one more story, a slightly different story, with different actors. Faculty members, as they talk over coffee in the faculty lounge, routinely trade stories and swap explanations of what goes on in their classes, why they succeed and why they so often fail. Our particular stories are not really out of the ordinary, and they elicited familiar explanatory lore from other teachers. The problem, they said, is . . . and proceeded to point the finger of blame, the only real issue being at whom it was to be pointed. Sometimes the problem was the students: their poor work habits, for instance, or academic deficiencies. "Maybe," remarked one colleague, "you're asking too much of them. Maybe they just can't cut it." Or, "Maybe their home situation is interfering." "Maybe they couldn't afford the book and didn't want to tell you," suggested another. Sometimes, more often, since community college faculty are so driven by a sense of service to students, the finger got pointed at the teacher. "You should really crack down on lateness," another colleague offered, and then said, try this. "You really have to be much clearer about your expectations" was commonly heard, accompanied by: try this. Our stories were thereby treated as cautionary tales, what can happen as a consequence of poor pedagogy, or improper classroom management. Overall, the recommendation was for us to give the students something they could succeed at, and accept that many of them would not do even that. Have them write the summaries that they were familiar with; let them sit silently and sullenly as long as they don't disrupt the class; be happy that they're coming at all, doing anything at all.

But isn't it true, someone might say, that our stories are hardly unique to community colleges? Haven't teachers always and everywhere been plagued by students not reading for class, not buying books, by their coming late, or not taking examinations seriously, by students trying collectively to persuade the teacher to ease up on requirements? Perhaps. But notice this critical difference: what is really interesting about our stories is less the bare facts, than what the students and teachers made of the facts.

What we as teacher took to be normal academic behavior was entirely delegitimated. What was peculiar was not that students did not do the reading, but rather that they could publicly challenge the appropriateness of the requirement that the reading be done. Not that students might initially fail at a more complex intellectual activity than they were used to, but that the teacher would be regarded with suspicion, and be publicly assailed for engaging in that activity. Not, finally, that students should together form an oppositional culture, but that the faculty should so much accede to its formation and maintenance. Those are the truly disturbing features of our three little stories.

What that suggests to us is that a promising way to understand the community college is as a distinctive academic culture. Within its classrooms faculty and students encounter and try to understand one another. They negotiate social norms, create forms of knowledge, modify their identities; they make meanings together. But in our examples the cultural exchanges between student and teachers have badly misfired. Students and teachers appear to disagree about the most basic, most mundane features of the classroom, as well as the larger vision of the nature and purpose of education,—whether being on time is important, for instance, or what counts as participation, what kinds of thought are valued, and whether any of it matters. Understanding the academic culture of community colleges, how and why it has come to be, how it gets sustained, and whether and how it might be reinvigorated—those are the goals of this book.

We began with our classroom stories because in them we see the problems of community colleges writ small. In our story of how community college professors make sense of them, we hear the traditional rhetoric and debates about community colleges, about open access, and, more globally, about the proper place of formal education within American society, the rhetoric and debates which characterized what has come to be called the movement for "democratic education."

For reformers in the first half of the twentieth century, the great work of democratic education was to be the creation of a universal system of mass education. The comprehensive high schools especially were to provide to the poor, and to minorities, genuine opportunity for social and economic advancement. The results of their efforts have been somewhat mixed. Universal education through secondary school, or at least compulsory attendance, has been a social fact for more than a half-century; but suspicion about the content and quality of that schooling has been with us almost as long. The democratic promise of education has been at best half realized, or badly compromised, as the nation evolved a dual system offering high quality to the privileged and a quite inferior education to poor and working-class children.

During the last twenty-five years the movement for democratic education shifted its emphasis from secondary to postsecondary education. Replaying the script that had produced the comprehensive high school, early efforts again were directed toward removing traditional barriers to access. This time the great triumph was the invention of the open-access college.

Although many large public colleges and universities are now either officially or effectively open access, by far the most representative are community colleges, for whom open access has been the guiding mission. At community colleges, "traditional" college students have been the rarity, have been so by design, a design that has hardly pleased everyone. Conservative legislators may complain that the urban and rural poor or working class, various ethnic minorities, displaced homemakers or the new unemployed, and the lowest achievers from high school can hardly be thought of as "college material"; still, that is the population with which open-access colleges are primarily concerned and for whom they exist.

From the beginning, the movement for democratic higher education was motivated by a palpable messianic fervor that helped shield open-access colleges from sustained scrutiny. But that fervor has dissipated under the pressure of hard reality—for teachers the daily classroom routine, for administrators the competitive scramble for scarcer public support. Now there must be real concern for the future of open-access institutions, real fear that they are falling along the familiar trajectory of educational reform: born in hopes and dreams, ending in cynicism and despair.

In the recent conservative era prominent government officials at all levels have publicly challenged the wisdom of open access, interpreting its troubles as failure, just one more failure of the liberalism of the 1960s. From their perspective an excessive concern for equality and opportunity eclipsed traditional commitment to excellence and high academic standards, quite predictably producing declining test scores, reduced academic achievement, and poor transfer rates. For such critics the central mission of open access was itself misguided. Pointing to the "masses," in "mass education," they sometimes asserted, sometimes suggested, that for whatever reasons of ability, or character, or personal history, they were markedly inappropriate college students. The millions of "nontraditional students" flocking to classrooms in open-access colleges, students whose backgrounds had not encouraged them toward, nor prepared them for a college education, should not be supported in college at public expense, but would be more properly diverted into vocational programs. On this account, open-access colleges should be much less like colleges, and much more like job training sites.

The political left has been critical of open-access institutions in a different way. Pointing to the institutions rather than the students, left critics don't see the problem with democratic higher education in its being impossible or wrongheaded but rather in its never really being attempted. Such critics have long contended that the open door is a "revolving door," that the publicly proclaimed mission of democratic education is only rhetoric behind which lurks the unpleasant reality of inferior institutions that offer only a debilitating education for the disadvantaged—all at the service of reinforcing the class structure of American society.

Critics from across the political spectrum naturally have very different notions about the ideal of mass public education, but they all see something deeply troubling about the reality. The current round of public reports and critical reflection has led to general acknowledgment that after a generation's efforts, open-access education has not yet proven successful. But the race may not have run its full course. Community colleges may yet, with energy and ingenuity, form themselves into powerful instruments for social equity and mobility, may yet overcome the historic dualism in education, may yet offer poor, minority, and other nontraditional students an education of substance and quality. For that to happen, however, community college faculty and administrators must learn to be more self-critical and reflective about their institutions than their political position encourages them to be.

Rethinking, reinventing the open-access college, while defending and preserving it, is bound to be a delicate task. That advocates of open access have not yet found a way to do it helps explain the peculiar public presentation of community colleges, their tendency to speak with two voices. One, the voice of defense and preservation, is loud and confident, emphasizing achievement—innovations such as learning labs, computer-assisted instruction, community sites, and, most importantly, the sustained commitment to the education of millions of nontraditional students who would otherwise never have been able to attend college.

But a second voice, muted, talks of tensions, dilemmas, and uncertainties, and insistently calls for reform.

In this second voice administrators speak of the severe decline in transfer rates, especially for minority and low-income students, of the difficulty in balancing traditional liberal arts transfer programs and vocational programs, and of maintaining the credibility of courses and credits as educational programs are redesigned in the direction of remediation. Faculty talk of the tensions and dissonances of their role. They relate their struggle to develop a professional identity in the face of institutional pressures to become more like trade school teachers than college professors, of creeping self-doubt as they compromise more and more, growing distant and detached from their disciplines. Most strikingly, for faculty initially attracted to the dream of democratic education, they tell of a daily sense of failure and futility, of hope lost.

This book attempts to understand and perhaps to unify the competing voices of community colleges. In it we acknowledge both the distance traveled and the distance still to go, both the important real achievements and the lingering problems that undercut those achievements.

Although our account is almost exclusively concerned with community colleges, both our analyses and recommendations have much broader implications. Community colleges have been the major entry point into higher education for the nontraditional students who have been the target of open access, but a broad range of colleges and universities now struggle with many of the same problems. Many traditional colleges faced with declining numbers of eighteen year-olds are now enrolling increasing numbers of nontraditional students; the community college's present offers one vision of their possible future. The problems first confronted by community colleges will soon be problems common to almost all of higher education, if they are not already.

Open access has been so much written and talked about that people require convincing that community colleges remain among the most misunderstood of institutions, routinely mischaracterized. Of course, almost everything about them is familiar in detail; quite ironically, that is the real source of the difficulty. Community colleges were relative latecomers as educational institutions. Their substantive administrative models and educational theories were drawn from institutions with quite different missions and resources. Partly they borrowed from universities, though they are not universities; from vocational schools, though they are not vocational schools; and from liberal arts colleges and high schools, though they are neither. Seeing so much that is familiar, almost anybody can think she understands community colleges, although almost nobody does.

Nor have they understood themselves particularly well either. Although they were the first to struggle with the problem of the "new students," they never fully came to grips with the meaning of that central experience, nor appreciated how historically novel was the effort to educate large numbers of nontraditional students, nor seen how that effort decisively changed the nature of teaching and learning within their classrooms and curricula.

Open-access colleges are almost always talked about in terms of a future, of their mission, what they are trying to accomplish. But, in fact, they can be understood only by exploring their past, by seeing how they have been changed by their success, by appreciating how their effort to educate nontraditional students has produced a distinctive academic culture, one reminiscent of those described in studies of the comprehensive high school—the earlier expression of the drive to open access. Books such as *The Shopping Mall High School* (Powell, Farrar, and Cohen, 1985) and *Horace's Compromise* (Sizer, 1984) show how the struggle to educate large numbers of extremely diverse students has had profound though unintended consequences, undermining the quality and altering the social meaning of education. The only comparable work for higher education to date is *Literacy in the Open-Access College* (Richardson, Fisk, and Okum, 1983), which tells a similarly disturbing story of declining standards, demoralized faculty, and poorly served students. For those committed to the ideal of democratic education, such studies should be read as setting the agenda for reform.

The difficulty that community colleges have in understanding themselves derives in part from how they have defined their mission. They have viewed themselves, and have been conceived by their major constituencies, as comprehensive institutions performing a variety of functions—remediation, community service, economic development, job training, career preparation, and transfer among others. As two-year institutions attempted to democratize education and serve new, nontraditional populations, most of the creative thought and innovation were channelled into these areas of their mission. The dramatic increase in the numbers and percentage of underprepared students brought the creation first of remedial and then of developmental programs, as well as a variety

of student academic and social support programs. The low rates of
college attendance and the serious life constraints of many nontraditional groups led to the explosive expansion of community-based
classes. Slowing economic growth in many regions coupled with
the need by employers for technical job training produced many
creative partnerships initiated by community colleges. All these
efforts produced a solid record of achievement.

During the innovative rush of the last generation the academic function alone was held to be unproblematic, as if that
would hold steady while everything around was in flux. But that
has turned out not to be the case. For now it is the nature, the
quality, the practice, and social meaning of academics that is vital
to the future of community colleges and their ability to serve the
next generation of nontraditional students. Certainly the "academic function" of community college is bound to be somewhat different from that of universities; the latter have a primary cultural
role in the preservation and expansion of knowledge. However, in
the important social role of preparing individuals for such careers
and professions which characteristically require the knowledge,
habits, and competencies of the rational disciplines, both make the
same promises, although community colleges make them to the
low-income and minority citizens for whom education historically
has been more a process of wedding out than a real invitation to
social advancement.

Paradoxically, it is precisely with respect to the academic
function, in which the promise made to nontraditional students is
so powerful while the distance to be crossed is so great, that we
find the least reflection on the nature of the problems of open access, and a peculiar reliance on traditional ideas. Community colleges, which think of themselves as innovative and creative, rely
heavily on university models of curriculum, education, departmental structure, and course content, while borrowing heavily from
secondary schools on matters of pedagogy. This dependence on familiar models has long delayed the examination of which curricular structures, educational environments, and teaching practices
are most effective in preparing nontraditional students for academic work.

So, posed most sharply, the central concerns of open-access
colleges are ultimately about academics, about whether academic
work can make a difference in the lives of nontraditional students. Can we take large numbers of students, many who have
failed in school in the past, who have little confidence in them-

selves, and help them develop strong academic abilities? Can we find ways to offer students not only access to higher education, in the sense of their being permitted to register for classes, but also in the more fundamental sense that their participation in higher education makes a real difference, offers them real opportunities, real prospects?

To be sure, not everyone believes that community colleges, or any educational institution, can have any important impact on the class structure of American society; perhaps the best that can be hoped for is only a limited meritocracy, a skimming. Certainly it could be argued that as originally conceived community colleges had extremely limited social goals, having been conceived as part of a movement toward the differentiation of higher education. In the 1920s many were founded primarily as low-cost alternatives to universities for less affluent students who, not coincidentally, were not expected to pursue professional careers, and so would not need the rigorous preparation the liberal arts provided in traditional four-year schools. This heritage, never completely overcome, continues to find expression in the competing voices of the community college. The loud, confident voice booms out education for all, while the softer and more troubled voice questions whether education should be the same for all, and wonders what open-access institutions can really promise their students.

Still, students have heard the promise of democratic education, even if it is really only a hope, and have tried to use the community college as a stepping-stone to new careers and new possibilities in their lives—which surely issues strong claims on our performance. If community colleges are to fulfill their responsibilities as nontraditional institutions, for nontraditional students whose aspirations they profit by and whose dreams they encourage, then ways must be found to be much more effective in the academic preparation of students. For, despite the characteristic penumbra of vocational, remedial, and social service programs, if community colleges are to be thought part of higher education at all, then the academic function must largely constitute their identity. If they are torn by a crisis of identity, by a speaking with two voices, then that is because of a fundamental distortion of the academic function, a weakening of the practices of academic life.

Indeed, the steady erosion of intellectual life in the open-access college is increasingly commented upon; and a conventional wisdom has already developed about how to reverse the spiral of decline. If students are unprepared for college classes then large,

precollege, or remedial programs can be made ever more prominent features of open-access colleges. If standards have dipped,
simply require more—by imposing a core curriculum, for example.
If teachers are caught in a cycle of burnout, cynicism, and despair,
various staff development practices can rekindle their enthusiasm
and retrain them in more appropriate pedagogy. And so on. But
how this particular array of diagnoses and remedies has come to
dominate in open-access colleges everywhere, and why it survives
and proliferates even in the face of failure: these are the issues we
have primarily set ourselves to understand. We believe the pale
educational practices that everywhere characterize the academic
culture of open-access colleges express the deep failure of educational theory to appreciate that education for nontraditional students cannot be just a weak version of education for the elite.

The story of open-access colleges is complicated, made more
so by the driving sense of social mission which leads them to be
forgetful of how they came to be and unmindful of how that history
shapes their possible future. We reconstruct their history in an
unusual way, primarily as intellectual and cultural history. For
this we draw on resources within interpretive social science, especially ethnography, cultural studies, and organizational theory,
combining an institutional history of the open-access college with
an account of the way the daily reality of teaching and learning
reenacts that history, and redeploys endlessly the stale vocabulary
and sterile educational theories associated with it. This combination of methods produces a novel picture of the open-access college,
a picture that makes sense of how they are experienced by teachers and students.

No illusions ought to be harbored as to the difficulty, unfa-
miliarity, and intricacy of the task of rethinking and reshaping the
academic culture of the open-access college. Nor should the level of
resistance to reform be underestimated; after all, staff have lived
their professional lives within easy and familiar categories and
structures. Whatever dissonances and dissatisfactions they experience have become the ordinary companions of their lives. But that
is just to notice what absolutely must be noticed—that institutional reform presents itself simultaneously as an abstract intellectual problem of understanding and as an intensely practical one
of action, either of which is ignored only at peril.

The second generation in any enterprise has the inevitable
advantage of historical perspective. Always, what appeared so
flawless in anticipation faces the review and assessment that nec-

essarily falls upon any great existing social institution—but this ought to be done respectfully, by way of reaffirming promises rather than reneging on them. So, our effort is Janus-faced, as it must be. One face looks to the past, taking seriously the history of institutions and reconstructing the great innovative movements and the self-understandings that motivated them. But the other face looks to the future, to roads not yet taken or even noticed.

The continuing problems with the reality of mass education, its apparent inability to cash in the promise of social mobility, is usually traced variously to failures of politics, or finances, or will. Without denying the importance and the power of such factors, we offer a new way to understand the trajectory of open-access colleges. For despite much money and good will, even during the period of liberal consensus, reform was routinely undercut by failure to develop, or even to notice the need to develop, an adequate theory of education for nontraditional students. The battle for access may have been won, especially if victory is understood in terms of numbers of students registering for classes. But the question that now has to be confronted is what access is access to. The battle for the rigor, substance, and distinctiveness, of community college education is the one that now must be fought.

THE PROBLEM
OF THE ACADEMIC CULTURE

Community colleges have not often appreciated the complexity of their own origins, and the deep tensions in their mission. Their great guidewords, "access" and "opportunity," are not really synonymous, although they are frequently taken to be; the gap between them looms wider as decades pass. Legislation, district policy, and board policy can decide the issue of access by dropping barriers to admission and by making adequate funding available. But opportunity is more than a matter of whether students get to sit in college classrooms; opportunity depends on what goes on in those classrooms. However, recent research raises disturbing questions about the academic rigor of the community college classrooms, and consequently, the real level of opportunity offered there.

In *Literacy in the Open-Access College,* Richard C. Richardson Jr., Elizabeth A. Fisk, and Morris A. Okum (1983) report on a three-year ethnographic study of a typical college within a large, multicampus community college system, "Oakwood." Their analysis is both novel and powerful. Rather than focusing on the standard fare—academic deficiencies of students or pedagogical failures of teachers—they look instead to the academic culture of the open-access college, particularly to the practice and social meaning of literacy. Their conclusion is that academic practices have gradually weakened at community colleges, that they have experienced a significant leveling down of the "norms of literacy."

Traditionally colleges had insisted upon what Richardson calls "texting." The comprehension and composition of sophisticated texts was very much at the heart of higher education, very prominent in the intellectual formation of students. Typically, they read books of the sort now called "primary sources" and wrote frequently in most of their courses. At open-access colleges, however, texting has been largely displaced by an impoverished form of linguistic behavior, "bitting." Bitting finds students reading textbooks, as opposed to primary texts, locating information, defining terms, and summarizing chapters. Evaluation primarily tests information retrieval. Examination devices such as true/false questions, fill in the blanks, and matching or multiple-choice questions, simply cue students to produce decontextualized, isolated, nonrhetorical, and fragmented language.

Since academic advancement and career mobility depend heavily upon sophisticated, critical, and expressive language use, the findings of the Richardson team are very unsettling. The academic culture that has come to pervade community colleges, they argue, plays strongly against the cultivation of the sorts of abilities most needed by students struggling to understand and to enter the academic and professional worlds.

Since institutions are naturally unwilling to engage in searching self-examinations, the impact of *Literacy in the Open-Access College* was severely limited. The implication that the reality of community college falls so far short of the ideal was enough to guarantee that the study be perceived as hostile. Although offered in a friendly way, the portrayal by Richardson and his associates raises issues which cannot be thought other than fundamental. If they are right, a profound irony in the history of community colleges is revealed: despite their commitment to democratic education, they come to delimit rather than enhance students' possibilities. How could that have happened despite a generation of talent and effort?

The story as told by the Richardson team is somewhat complicated, since it proceeds at various levels—from classroom teacher to chancellor. With sweeping strokes, the narrative traces shifting classroom expectations and pedagogical practices back to broad policy decisions at the district level, and the manner in which those policies were translated into specific organizational goals at individual campuses. The decision to expand enrollment was made at the highest levels. On individual campuses that meant underprepared students, large numbers of them, whose presence put great stress on the existing curriculum and support services. At the same time district attempts to reduce costs brought an increased reliance on part-time faculty—a practice which tended increasingly to isolate faculty in their classrooms and reduce collegiate control over the curriculum. Finally, faculty members, lacking both the means to dramatically improve student skills and the authority to maintain traditional expectations, informally "renegotiate" with students classroom relations, academic norms, and intellectual practices.

The attenuation of course content, expectations, and requirements result from the meeting of nontraditional students with a traditional faculty, ill-prepared, as anyone would be, for this novel educational setting. On the student side of the desk are mostly what Richardson calls "requirement meeters" and "specific or nonspecific information users"; on the teacher side are instructors whose pedagogical goals are the limited cognitive objectives of information dissemination.

In retrospect the accommodations made by each side, the inevitable *modus vivendi*, perhaps ought to have been foreseeable. As the average level of academic preparedness and interest of students declines, the faculty—committed to a particular instructional style, the classroom lecture, and a limited instructional goal, "information transfer"—respond by simply watering down the requirements. They both transfer less complex information to the students via lectures and demand much less literate behavior from the students by replacing term papers and essays, for instance, with check marks on multiple-choice exams. What begins in the individual classroom ultimately alters the entire intellectual climate of the school; throughout, the norms of literate activity gradually dip, as the rigor of academic work is negotiated away.

The intellectual drift described in *Literacy in the Open Access College* is not a function of open access *per se*. But it does appear to be what happens what open access is unguided by an adequate understanding of nontraditional education. This is not peculiar to community colleges; it has happened before. Studies reveal mass secondary education to be beset by similar difficulties in maintaining a strong academic culture. Particularly valuable is the ethnographic study of high schools reported by Arthur Powell, Eleanor Farrar, and David Cohen in *The Shopping Mall High School* (1985). Their remarkable central metaphor, the "shopping mall high school," captures the fact that both the public comprehensive high school and the shopping mall are primarily characterized by practices directed at inclusiveness—to serve as many people as possible, to provide something for everyone, to cater to consumer choice. Their analysis roughly parallels that of the Richardson group; the ground level consequences of the commitment to inclusiveness are traced throughout the high school—its formal administrative structure and extensive array of student services, to be sure, but also its cultural features, particularly the pedagogies and academic practices that evolve among teachers and students.

Because the high school curriculum is shaped by the desire to retain as many students as possible, it has become differentiated to an extraordinary degree; in fact, "the word 'curriculum' does not do justice to the astonishing variety that one finds" (Powell et al., 1985:2). The broad "horizontal" curriculum is hard to miss: from anatomy to zoology, from science to science fiction, from art to the art of cooking, almost any course for almost any interest. The curriculum is also arranged "vertically." Sections of what look like the same course, which carry the same course title or description, say composition or American history, may actually differ quite dramatically from one another. Within the same high school, what counts as American literature, for instance, may include courses which have students reading a demanding list of major primary texts, but may also include courses which teach literature through comic strips, courses which are designed for students who are not expected to be able or willing to do any reading for the course. The spacial imagery of verticality may be a bit misleading; it encourages thinking in terms of varying levels of difficulty, but in fact differences among courses in the vertical curriculum are differences in kind as well as in intensity. "Levels" are not so much a matter of how hard material is, or how much of it students will have to master, as they are a matter of different sorts of expectations, of changes in the nature of the activities students undertake.

The complicated differentiation of the secondary school curriculum, with its proliferation of courses both horizontally and vertically—perhaps hundreds of courses, each at multiple levels—inevitably has had unanticipated repercussions for the academic culture. The curriculum has so many options that it serves to dilute the school's responsibility to its students; choices come to rest almost entirely on the student and her family. The high school simply offers the choice; it remains neutral itself, even indifferent, about what selection is made. Schools "will press themselves to offer great variety but will not press students to choose wisely or engage deeply—it is a deliberate approach to accommodating diversity so that students will stay on, graduate, and be happy" (Powell et al., 1985:2). Although students will say "You can get a good education here if you want it," that is not accompanied by any sense that faculty or administrators expect students to follow a demanding and intellectually rigorous academic program. Similarly, faculty feel little pressure to reach substantive agreements among themselves about educational goals or the expectations they should have of students. The academic community among the staff has become so weakened that "community has come to mean differences peacefully coexisting rather than people working together toward some serious end" (Powell et al., 1985:3).

Inside ordinary "shopping mall" classrooms informal negotiation really determines the processes, the content, even the goals of individual courses. In the absence of institutional guidance or expectations, students and teachers strike bargains—"classroom treaties"—which decide the features of students' classroom experience: the kind of and intensity of engagement with, or avoidance of learning, the sort of relations students have with teachers and with one another, the amount of time committed to various learning activities, and the degree of seriousness that is brought to academic work. Thus, "a course may require more time or less time. Personal relationships may be employed to relate to the subject or to ignore it. A teaching method may approach the subject intensively or passively. Participation in class carries no general expectations for either students or teachers" (Powell et al., 1985:117). Where classroom treaties are the norm, high schools have seen the legitimation of a tremendous variety of learning environments. Many classes expect little commitment or effort from students and provide only meager models of intellectual activity. Others may provide a richer academic setting, but the important point is that as far as the school is concerned all options are equally available, and equally proper. The aspect that such schools present to students, and to faculty, is neutrality and indifference about the nature and worth of the academic enterprise.

This picture of the comprehensive high school is reminiscent of the Richardson group's portrayal of the academic culture of community colleges; nor should it be surprising that the two great institutional efforts at democratic education have travelled down similar roads. If neither has yet found how to translate open access into substantive opportunity, perhaps that is because they were not really designed to that end. As David Cohen argues in the latter part of *The Shopping Mall High School,* current curricular structures and classroom practices should not be thought of as attempts to solve the problems of democratic education. They have a much more ambiguous status as the heritage or remnants of the great debates about whether to try for democratic education at all.

Beginning in the 1890s, high school enrollments doubled each decade as growing numbers of immigrant children entered formal schooling; the new experience of mass secondary education was accompanied by stormy, public debate about the nature of the high school, its curriculum, pedagogy, and goals. Although lines of argument crisscrossed and intertwined, the disputants divided into three main camps, with advocates of the traditional classical curriculum cast into a defensive fight against two distinct thrusts for reform. Harvard's innovative president, Charles W. Eliot, pressed to reshape curricula in ways that would emphasize study of modern subjects, such as mathematics and science, while providing students more elective choice. Others, led by G. Stanley Hall of Clark University, argued for a curriculum geared to the needs of the majority of students who could not be expected to have an interest in or much capacity for academic work. Debate was joined on several issues, but the central question was whether all students should pursue an intellectually demanding program of academic study, or whether they should follow an easier and more "practical" curriculum. The familiar compromise solution was to do both, to develop a dual educational system in which a small minority of college-bound students are provided a rigorous academic program while the bulk of students are provided a rigorous academic program while the bulk of students pursue a curriculum designed for those less able or less interested in academic work (Powell, et al., 1985:239-253; Krug, 1972; Kimball, 1986). This somewhat ambiguous commitment to democracy and education for all, within a system of dual expectations, was emphasized and codified in what became the bible of school reformers, the 1918 NEA report, *Cardinal Principles of Secondary Education*.

By the 1930s the new, and by now familiar, system of mass public education was firmly in place. It featured a few broad curricular tracks which distinguished the rigorously trained college-bound from the great majority of students for whom academic demands had been eased. The latter were served by practical, vocational, and personal development programs, supported by an extensive extracurriculum of sports and clubs. Radically different conceptions of academic work and standards of academic performance were thereby institutionalized; overall, a climate was established in the schools which discouraged serious academic work, and which highlighted instead the social and practical dimensions of school.

The worlds of high schools and colleges are often thought far apart; nevertheless, the story of modern comprehensive high schools provides a valuable way to think about contemporary community colleges. As the later stage of the same struggle for democratic education, community colleges share the intellectual history of the "great school debates"; they appropriated for their work the terms legitimated there and have even rediscovered and replayed the same organizational and curricular options. Although recent fashionable arguments of E. D. Hirsch (1987) and Allan Bloom (1987) depend heavily upon the imagery of a golden age of hardworking students and intellectually demanding schools from which we've declined (and even Richardson talks of the "leveling down" of community colleges), that is simply not the case. Actually, contemporary curricula and pedagogical practices have been shaped by prior efforts at reform that attempted to deal with much the same issues in much the same ways.

The important point to take from the two studies we have canvassed is that what look like multiple discrete features of educational institutions actually come as a package. Organizational and curricular structures may seem to vary independently, each in turn independent from the vocabulary in which an institution describes and understands itself. But in fact those are all mutually constraining, and only really intelligible in relation to one another within institutional history. Taken together they guarantee that what is called "reform" will be a continually driving feature of educational institutions—as long as reform comes in the approved species, as the insistence that schools do well but not enough. Reformers rarely draw the lesson that failed practice discloses failed theory, that reform should be more than a matter of proliferating offices and expanding activities, more than refining and baroquing courses, programs, structures. Implementation may be thought a problem, or the students intractable, but not that mass education has been continually replaying the great school debates in the daily classroom experience of students. The uncomfortable and long-avoided conclusion is that substantial alteration in the outcomes of comprehensive, open-access institutions is not a problem of will, which has been good and enough, but of understanding, of finding perspicacious ways of seeing differently what we now see conventionally and unreflectively.

College in the Era of Disarticulation

As community colleges gradually accommodated themselves to a generation of "new," or nontraditional students, they evolved

22   The Academic Crisis of the Community College

away from many of the traditional mores of higher education. Curricular structures, for instance, were reshaped, as shifting student demographics appeared as a pronounced alteration in course-taking patterns. Increasingly, community college students were part-time, frequently episodic course-takers, professedly less interested in degress. Most community colleges are enrollment driven: they have been extremely sensitive to patterns of student choice. Consequently, such changes eroded traditional curricular structures and degree-granting programs, the Associates in Arts, for example, and encouraged an unprecedented expansion of curricula with few formal requirements. In some community colleges such a "shopping mall," or "cafeteria," curricula can contain fully half the student body, with the rest mostly in highly structured vocational programs.

That kind of hard data aside, nontraditional students have remained mysterious, although major analysts of community colleges all have attempted to characterize their distinctiveness and to understand the challenge they present. K. Patricia Cross described them as new to higher education because only in an age of open admissions would they be considered "college material." About two-thirds were first generation college-goers; in traditional measures of academic achievement, most ranked in the lowest third of high school graduates (Cross, 1971:6). Together with other influential theorists such as John Roueche, Arthur Cohen, and Florence Brawer, she argued throughout the 1960s and 1970s that such students could never be effectively served by watered-down versions of regular college courses, nor by traditional pedagogies. What was needed, they each claimed, was an instructional revolution based on the principles of mastery learning, and the individualization of instruction made possible by development of new learning technologies. More recently, Dale Parnell described the natural community college clientele as that "great mass of individuals in the middle quintiles of the typical high school student body." His recommendation was to develop innovative degree programs that blend liberal arts with technical education (Parnell, 1985:16).

All major first generation theorists were concerned with devising curricular structures and instructional processes appropriate to the extremely diverse group of nontraditional students who previously had experienced only limited academic success. They agreed that community colleges would have to break from conventional university conceptions of curriculum and instruction, and find unconventional, nontraditional ways to work with nontraditional students. Unfortunately, since they were so influential in determining the general direction in which innovation was pursued and solutions sought, they shared a somewhat conventional view of the unconventional. They construed the problem of nontraditionality primarily in terms of individual cognitive psychology; the solution was to be the nuanced, individualized application of educational technology.

Perhaps it is more fruitful to conceive education in cultural rather than psychological terms. The understandings, motivations, and practices of students and faculty may be better thought of as shaped by distinctive institutional contexts and relationships, than as invariant functions of the structure of the brain. Sociologists, of course, have been arguing that point for a long time. David Riesman, for instance, suggested that colleges and universities can be sorted by the extent students identify with the value system of the faculty. His sketch of the structure of higher education located the elite private colleges and universities at the top, followed by flagship state universities, through the other types of schools which display increasing divergence between the values of faculty and students (Riesman, 1980).

Of course, college students have always varied in their degree of acceptance of faculty values and their willingness to subordinate themselves to the goals of the curriculum. And, historian Helen Horowitz has shown that the current cultural configuration is not of long standing. College life of the last century valued irresponsibility, good humor, and carefree abandon; it revolved around the extracurriculum of fraternities, athletics, clubs. The "college man" rejected the formal academic curriculum, in favor of the extracurriculum, believing business and professional success to depend less on mastering academics, and more on demonstrating leadership, developing personal style, and forging contacts. Only a minority of students acceded authority to the faculty and formed a culture oppositional to college life. Horowitz calls them "outsiders" (Horowitz, 1987).

Those nineteenth-century attitudes toward academic life echo still. However, Horowitz argues, early in this century the informal, antagonistic college life of undergraduates was-co-opted into the formal institutional life of colleges. The Greek system was accepted; athletics were subsidized and directed by faculty/coaches; secret societies were reborn as honor societies. Simultaneously, growth and formalization of the professions, and changing notions of the path to economic success, were reflected in the incorporation within college life of the outsider culture of hard work, diligence, and grade consciousness.

Despite qualifications of the sort noticed by Horowitz, until the massive expansion of higher education in the 1960s, students and faculty shared similar backgrounds and life-worlds, and enacted familiar cultural roles. The most stereotypically "collegiate" students, striving only for "gentleman's C's," understood the value system they were rejecting by engaging in the social rather than the intellectual life of the college. The value systems of students and faculty were in at least rough articulation. This fact deeply shaped the teaching and learning situation of traditional institutions since it assured mutual understanding and working agreement about the aims of the curriculum and the value of such academic practices as writing, interpretation, argumentation, and analysis. But the very success of the original mission of the community college, the democratization of education, access, has shattered the once routine expectation that teachers and students share a common cultural world.

The educational problem of nontraditionality is not really primarily a problem of low skills, or spotty previous high school achievement, or low income, or family responsibilities. More centrally it is what sociologists call a "structural disarticulation" between colleges and their student populations. Even very bright community college students, and there are many, are nontraditional in the sense that they typically carry a spectacularly nonstandard repertoire of behaviors and attitudes with which to cope with the traditional requirements of college life. Overwhelmingly, they come from backgrounds which have not prepared them to identify with, or even to recognize the central values and practices of academic life, and which have not provided adequate models of intellectual activity. They do not take themselves seriously as learners of something worth learning, but rather view themselves as engaged in a certification process in which credits are "accumulated," and requirements as unreasonable obstacles placed in their path. Often they come from backgrounds which do not value controversy and debate, so that they tend to reduce reasoned inquiry and principled dispute to just "matters of opinion." Many, also, have little sense of controlling their lives; they see themselves as having little command of the resources that might improve their prospects.

The cultural disarticulation that is the central feature of open-access colleges has been noticed by major ethnographic studies where it appears as the social psychology of disarticulation. For instance, in the late 1970s, Howard London reported on his study of a newly founded urban community college that served predominantly white working-class students (London, 1978). He argued that the students were deeply ambivalent toward themselves and their situation. In his account, the students had internalized an individualistic ideology which traces academic success to character traits such as hard work, diligence, and self-discipline. But acceptance of such a characterological account of success naturally produces self-doubts in students who previously had been mostly unsuccessful in school. Since the traditional nostrums—be disciplined, work harder, and so on—have not worked for them in the past, academic competence seems frustratingly out of reach, mysterious, and, students fear, unattainable. To protect their self-worth and dignity, students adopt a defensive stance. Then they are caught in a double bind. The students suspect their own ability to do intellectual work, to handle ideas and language, yet still they hold them to be important, indeed as indicators of personal worth. The ability to engage in abstract reasoning, and to handle language carefully are, they believe, essential for success in the world and for entry into the middle class, and failure to master those abilities is potentially crushing to their sense of self and their hopes for the future. Thus, according to London, for community college students intellectual activity is simultaneously alluring, but emotionally charged, and deeply problematic.

With such complex feelings rarely acknowledged, the classroom becomes dangerous terrain, dealing with teachers fraught with tension and anxiety. Each classroom is the scene of negotiation between the teacher and the students. Teachers, for their part, cannot begin a course assuming that students will be committed to the work, or will even come regularly, appear for examinations, or turn in assignments. London, like Lois Weis in her more recent study of a community college serving primarily black, low-income students, describes a familiar situation in which students drop in and out of school, arrive late, and too frequently exert little effort (Weis, 1985). Students have great difficulty seeing school as a comfortable, inviting environment. In the case of the exchange between vocational program students and the liberal arts faculty, London found the most striking instances of barely muted conflict. Here was the least agreement about the nature and level of expectations; consequently, those classes were most likely to trigger student fears and ambivalences. Here, particularly, academic work has the dual quality of attractiveness and danger.

The prevalent, indeed, canonical, understandings of educational psychology and student services make it extremely difficult to recognize the social and cultural dimensions of the disarticulation between nontraditional students and academic life; but seeing the ways student culture intersects, or fails to intersect academic practice and expectation, throws the educational issues into sharp relief. The hard job is not just to build student skills or provide them with information but to create a learning context which alters students' sense of the nature of intellectual life, their conception of themselves as learners, and their fundamental orientation to academic practices. For that, movement on both sides of the desk is needed, since students already carrying a rich cultural ensemble cannot magically transform themselves into traditional students. And, even if they could, community colleges have not held still. If the Richardson team is correct, colleges themselves have evolved away from being traditional academic institutions, partly by choice, and partly through diffuse efforts to accommodate nontraditionality through informal negotiation.

Education as a Social Act

Nontraditionality is usually talked about as if carried inside the heads and hearts of individual students, rather than being characteristic of student *populations*. It holds place for what are thought to be cognitive and affective deficiencies, the social features of nontraditionality being quite invisible inside canonical cognitive psychology. Once the phenomenon of cultural disarticulation has been noticed, however, new disciplinary resources can be brought to bear which yield a rich picture of the striking mismatch between nontraditional students and academic life. For instance, recent work in composition theory and literary criticism suggests how to understand the complex relations among nontraditionality, declining norms of literacy, and the practices of the academic culture.

The contemporary theoretical work itself is necessarily somewhat arcane. But what it comes to is that scholars studying the processes of interpretation and understanding among readers and writers in a literate community have come to reject context invariance of meaning, in favor of theories that emphasize the crucial historical and cultural dimensions of meaning and thought. The prominent composition theorist, David Bartholomae, who has written extensively on remediation, sees the dramatic implications of such research for understanding nontraditional students:

Every time a student sits down to write for us, he has to invent the university for the occasion—invent the university, that is, or a branch of it, like history or anthropology or economics or English. The student has to learn to speak our language, to speak as we do, to try on the peculiar ways of knowing, selecting, evaluating, reporting, concluding, and arguing that define the discourse of our community. Or perhaps I should say the various discourses of our community . . . or the student must try on a variety of voices and interpretive schemes—to write as a literary critic one day and as an experimental psychologist the next; to work within fields where the rules governing the presentation of examples or the development of an argument are both distinct and, even to a professional mysterious (Bartholomae, 1985:134).

In Bartholomae's provocative metaphor, students who undertake academic reading and writing must "invent the university" by identifying and decoding, perhaps constructing for themselves, its characteristic forms of thought and analysis. Writing, thought also, are essentially social and rhetorical, rather than introspective, expressive, or private. Student writers are therefore social actors whose immediate problem is situating themselves appropriately within academic discourse communities. That rhetorical act can misfire in different and unsuspected ways. For instance, students are often encouraged to think of their audience as the course instructor, but Bartholomae sees that the casual identification of instructor with audience is misleading and pernicious. If the university is to be intelligible to the uninitiated, to students, individual instructors must stand for something beyond themselves. Sociologists or historians who are just peculiar or eccentric figures have no call on the respective attention of students. That comes only when individual instructors represent to students the complex cultural phenomena that are their disciplines, with the rich traditions and distinctive methods that bind the membership. Even for so-called "basic writers," learning to write involves much more than mastering the mechanics of grammatical structure and punctuation, or logic. By far the more significant achievement is appreciating the essentially rhetorical nature of writing and thought. "Inventing the university" means recognizing not one single set of styles and standards. Each discipline, and certainly each cluster such as the natural or social sciences, comprise distinct "disciplinary cultures" which have their own complex, implicit standards of analysis, description, and argumentation which enable disciplinary discourse, and constrain it (Geertz, 1983).

In *Is There a Text in This Class?*, literary theorist Stanley Fish makes a quite similar case concerning how readers interpret and discuss texts.

> Communication occurs only *within* . . . a context or situation or interpretive community and the understanding achieved by two or more persons is specific to that context . . . to be in a situation is already to be in possession of a structure of assumptions, [to share a background] of practices, purposes, goals (Fish, 1980: 304 and 318).

The meaning of any text is not objectively embedded in it; meaning is constructed by the interpretive practices of competent readers who select among and organize aspects of the text. Bartholomae saw that being a competent writer requires mastery of appropriate disciplinary conventions; so also, Fish sees that being a competent reader requires mastery of interpretive strategies for each discipline or "interpretive community." Thus, literacy is primarily a social achievement—understanding and emulating the conventions of discourse communities—rather than a purely linguistic or cognitive psychological phenomenon.

When literacy is understood in that way standard pedagogical issues are recast. Inevitably, interpretation is multiple and uncertain, meaning fragile. Making sense of texts and disciplines of thought constructed according to unfamiliar rules, and shaped by alien concerns, is sure to be terribly difficult. But it is the educational task faced by college students, most especially nontraditional college students—to think, talk, and argue within the various academic discourse communities, as historians, for example, or biologists, or psychologists.

A student's academic career consists of a series of initiations into different, somewhat loosely related, intellectual, and cultural communities, each with its own norms of discourse, its special vocabulary and set of important questions. A successful college student is one who manages to puzzle out what is distinctive about the various disciplines she encounters, and grasps the overall configuration of the educational enterprise in which she is engaged. Even the best-prepared, most highly motivated college students may be frustrated navigating among diverse disciplines with disparate styles of rational inquiry. That is a normal, expected feature of a student's experience (Perry, 1970). However, nothing in the background of nontraditional students has prepared them for it. In almost every way college seems more alien and hostile to them, unsympathetic to the ways they have brought with them from their home communities or social class. About that they are entirely correct. Especially for them, college demands not just intellectual growth but also social and cultural transformations that are profoundly bewildering and unsettling.

The ordinary psychological features of the transition to college life are detailed by Vincent Tinto in his research on student retention. A student's college career, he argues, should really be seen as movement from membership in a home community to membership in a college community. If all goes well this will follow a familiar pattern of separation, transition, and incorporation (Tinto, 1987;1988). To achieve full incorporation into the social and intellectual life of a college, students must separate themselves, or at least distance themselves, from prior associations. Obviously, not everybody makes the transition. Whether or not a particular student does depends on a number of factors: the character of the home community, its views on the worth of schooling, and the extent to which college is seen as a normal stage in the life cycle. Successful students are those who complete the social and cultural transition. Students who never fully incorporate into the new community typically fail or drop out.

The processes of separation, transition, and incorporation will be unpredictable and trying for most students—but nontraditional students experience the greatest struggle. For them, particularly, the transition to college is a stressful and threatening process of shifting membership and renegotiating identify. It may be most arduous for minority students. Black males have shown the greatest decline in college participation (Nettles, 1988; Mingle, 1987); they are very likely to have come from backgrounds which led them to doubt their abilities and to encourage "getting-over" as an academic strategy (Saufley, Cowan, and Blake, 1983). Black students also report the greatest difficulty coping with cultural features of college—such as the social distance between students and teachers, and relatively detached teaching styles—which they often find slighting (Nettles, 1988). However, nontraditional students all are similarly outsiders to college life, and tend not to think of themselves as persons who will do well academically.

Higher education is daunting for nontraditional students because the culture of academics is foreign and mysterious to them.

But there is no royal road around it: initiation into the multiple intellectual worlds that comprise academic life is still required for successful educational and professional careers. The educational challenge for community colleges is the construction of bridges of understanding across which students may move from nontraditional backgrounds to competent membership in the educated community. Traditional university models of curriculum and pedagogy are not helpful. Since they obscure the initiatory and transformative aspects of education, they may actually be harmful. Curricular forms and teaching practices can't be thought to be culturally neutral instruments, which mean the same to all people. They enact a specific form of life; more than telling about academic and professional life, they represent, show it. Debased practices may falsify, or misrepresent it.

Literacy in the Open-Access College portrays bitting practices as a watering down of the usual academic work of the university. Actually they are more interesting than that, more harmful. Bitting doesn't just reduce academic requirements; it fundamentally changes them, and consequently misrepresents intellectual practices. Bitted disciplines appear as mere compilations of facts, strung together by discrete concepts within a transparent theory. The complex culture of disciplines, their theoretical and cognitive aspects, as well as their social and rhetorical dimensions, are all hidden, or denied.

Although it is easy enough to see how such practices inhibit students' initiation into academic life, the easy and obvious alternatives may not be really any better—indeed, as their easiness and obviousness ought to have signalled to us. For example, the Richardson group recommends texting as a prominent instructional mode. And recently there have been many calls for faculty to move away from lecture and recitation as their basic teaching style, to move from "teaching as talking to," to teaching that engages and involves students, which encourages active rather than passive learning. From the perspective we are adopting, that education for nontraditional student is actually an initiation, a social and cultural transformation, such recommendations at least look suspicious. After all, bitting may be fun. What is called "engagement" and "involvement" may come to nothing more than classroom excitement, though of course they may be much more. "Active" learning may be of trivialities; in fact the whole arsenal of progressivist and reformist educational jargon has long been set at the service of whatever pedagogy anyone cares to push.

Almost all reformers now concur in rejecting the straight lecture course, accompanied by a textbook to be memorized. But discussion groups, "inquiry," "discovery," and "writing across the curriculum"—the standard range of alternatives—all focus attention primarily at the level of individual student psychology: they also fail to confront the cultural features of the exchange between nontraditional students and the evolving academic culture of open-access colleges. We will have much to say about curriculum and teaching, but all of it returns ultimately to this set of issues—the nature of nontaditionality, what academic culture pervades open-access institutions, how academic and intellectual life is represented in practice, and what initiatory or transformative processes are provided to students.

The problems of mass public education are so deeply rooted and long standing that by now the failures of comprehensive and open-access schools can hardly be thought accidental or anomalous. No quick and easy fix is possible, nor leave untouched most structures and practices while focusing on a supposed recalcitrant few. However, while educational reform is certain to be difficult and perhaps painful, it is not impossible. What makes it seem impossible is that so long as issues are framed in the familiar ways, and routinely dropped in the area of responsibility of the familiar offices, all that can reasonably be expected are the familiar outcomes. The hardest part about successful institutional reform is finding ways to reframe the familiar, and for that contemporary organizational theory provides a valuable guide.

The Organizational Culture of Open Access

The principal insight of contemporary organizational theory is that although organizations may be conceived as if typically engaged in the constant careful adjustment of means to ends, their members certainly are not such pure rational actors whose actions and interactions are governed by calculation of self-interest. To the contrary, behavior at all levels of an organization, including management, is continuously and silently shaped by a pervasive organizational culture which provides the social and conceptual environment in which action can be meaningfully conceived. Consequently, organizations always elude complete managerial control; paradoxically, they are more adaptive and effective, managers more in control, when the limits of direct control are grasped. If actions of the organization, its policies and structures, for instance, and within the organization, the ordinary practices of its members, are thought of as artifacts which express and embody a shared culture, then the powerful resources of contemporary cultural sciences can be invoked to understand them and to chart strategies for change.

Earlier functionalist conceptions of organizational behavior conceived it as a set of learned responses to external problems in the environment. The new organizational theorists draw heavily from recent "postfunctionalist" social science; they emphasize instead the symbolic nature of culture, and the primacy of the language-like. Meaning is experienced and expressed within public vehicles such as rituals and ceremonies, but also in the privacy of individual minds, each shaped by cultural categories and patterns of inference and legitimation. Participants in a culture unconsciously appropriate, more or less fully, those available forms of life, modes of understanding, and strategies for action (Swidler, 1986). Effective management of organizational change therefore is an extremely subtle and complicated affair, calling more for an anthropological turn of mind than a bureaucratic one.

Organizations and institutions are dynamic; but their modes of change are usually best appreciated retrospectively. It is a commonplace that intervention within organizations hardly ever has the desired effect, that institutions adapt to initiatives for change with quietly powerful and effective "normalizing" resistance. Attempts to guide the development of large institutions that play within the framework of the accepted argot are particularly susceptible to co-option. Much more promising are efforts that start by recognizing that organizational culture seeks always to maintain itself—and this is as true for community colleges as it is for business firms.

The greatest obstacle to guided change is that organizational culture, as any culture, is naturally invisible to the natives, for whom it operates as a transparent framework of meaning. However, a cultural analysis can suggest change at levels deeper than ordinary reform because it sees more deeply, and can disclose hidden relations of thinking, talking, and acting. When a culture is thus brought to consciousness, then it may be acted upon as well as acted within. Perhaps, if care is exercised, it may even be changed.

Obviously, the fine detailing of a culture, what the anthropologist Clifford Geertz calls a "thick description" (Geertz, 1973), can be an extremely powerful resource. What anthropologists have, which ordinary managers don't have, but organizational theorists recommend they get, is a theoretical perspective broad enough and language rich enough to permit thick description. This kind of activity will seem simultaneously puzzling and familiar, possibly hostile, to insiders of the organization, since it proposes to think and talk about everyday practices and concerns in ways that make them intelligible to an outsider. Put somewhat differently, the object of disclosure is what seems most unproblematic from within, namely, how the culture thinks and talks about itself.

This is the perspective from which we look at the cluster of issues that collectively comprise the problem of the academic culture. We accept that new styles of understanding are bound to seem unnecessarily arcane and irritating for so long as they lack the benefits of familiarity. Certainly, many people would be happier if at least the long-standing problem definitions and their associated well-known solution sets were left inviolate—the jolt of having to reconceive the central problematics of one's profession should not be underestimated. Others will see interpretive cultural methods as offering a strategy for cutting through dreary dichotomies and played out debates. "Redescription" may empower institutions that have been paralysed by their own unreflective discourse and practices. Self-conscious and self-guided reform is always less likely than sporadic, incremental, and episodic accommodation to outside pressures or to occasional dimly perceived crises. But demystifying the institutional mythos, unpacking the intricate ways that underlying conceptions play themselves out in hard reality, offers new openings for action at all levels of the community college system—to policymakers, administrators, and faculty members.

The sociologist Peter Berger remarks that the social sciences inevitably have a "debunking" quality: the most treasured features of particular social roles can be "seen through" easily by persons not entangled in the system. From the outside, for instance, it is not hard to see that faculty labor under the illusion of autonomy. Isolated in their classrooms, individual faculty members believe themselves completely free to develop innovative teaching approaches, that they can experiment as they will. Ordinary institutional categories encourage that belief, favorably contrasting it with curriculum "imposed" from above. Nevertheless, perceived autonomy is constrained both by institutional structure and organizational culture, neither of which can be eluded by teachers or students. An obvious example of a structural constraint is the requirement that educational activities must conform to the exigencies of crediting. Education proceeds everywhere through the vehicle of the three credit course. Faculty members have so internalized that constraint that they are long past noticing that it is a constraint, thinking it part of the natural order of things. Later we will argue that the relative isolation and independence of faculty members under conditions of severe structural constraint is an important ingredient in the creation of an anemic academic culture. Similarly, administrators are caught within the illusion of formal structure; their reality comprises the formal and easily quantifiable elements of teaching and learning—FTEs, program completion rates, and course objectives. They naturally will have difficulty understanding either the informal negotiations which shape classrooms or the wider sets of attitudes and expectations that constitute the academic culture.

Those examples are enough to show the curious paradox of ethnographically based policy analysis. Within any culture the range of opportunity will always seem constricted by powers too great to challenge. The most subtle and powerful constraints are its own categories and predilections; unless policy recommendations are couched in those ordinary terms they will appear alien, unsympathetic, and simply unavailable. On the other hand, recommendations clothed in familiar garb elicit perfectly predictable responses, well-known and oft-tried moves. For example, once the issue of transfer education is talked about in terms of "articulation" or "credit accumulation," only so many options are really open, none of which will be strikingly innovative.

Such appears to have been the fate of the recommendations in *Literacy and the Open-Access College*. Recognizing the complexity of the institutional picture they had sketched, Richardson and his associates proposed an assortment of conventional policy options—more selective recruiting, for example, or giving financial aid only to those students pursuing academic degrees, and carefully defining academic progress. These suggestions, if not rejected outright by community college administrators and policymakers, have at least generated little enthusiasm. Institutions which self-define so strongly as inclusionary, see little merit in exclusionary practices of any kind, whenever implemented and however masked.

Less conventional recommendations from the Richardson group which were more closely tied to their distinctive ethnographic findings apparently were deemed immediately out of bounds and received little attention. A very striking example is the recommendation that colleges reduce their substantial reliance on part-time faculty. This is one of those perennial issues on which almost everything that can be said has been said, at least within the familiar lines of debate. For administrators the issue of part-time staffing is primarily a matter of fiscal responsibility and administrative flexibility, secondarily matters of anticipated employee commitment or quality control. Except that part-timers teach only one or two courses per semester, they are from a formal managerial perspective identical to their full-time colleagues. Given adequate credentials and common course objective, adjuncts can be expected to teach roughly as well, and at very significant savings to the institutions. For full-time faculty, and their unions, the practice of large-scale staffing with part-time instructors appears more ominous, although their objections flow from a parallel misunderstanding of the college. They allege lower individual commitment of part-timers, question the level of effort and involvement she can be expected to make in the classroom. Just as administrators see the practice as benign because of their focus on the formal features of instruction, so faculty view it as harmful because of their belief in the autonomy of the classroom instructor and the significance that lends to the moral and affective qualities of individual instructors. Neither administers nor faculty recognize the cultural implications of staffing patterns; both portray college as students, one by one, interacting with faculty, one by one.

When an organizational theorist or an ethnographer sees a practice so widespread, she puts a very different cast to it than either administrators or faculty. For staffing with part-time instructors to seem so natural and inevitable, individual courses in the curriculum have to be conceived as relating to one another somewhat loosely. Faculty members have to appear as jobbers in their courses, bearing only such relations to one another as journeymen within a guild. As the college faculty is but an aggregate, the curriculum is summative. Students are not thought to relate to the faculty as a group or to the college as a whole, but rather to individual teachers within individual courses which are taken one by one, perhaps, at most, "sequenced." Colleges are even fiscally organized according to a fragmented and atomized notion of their academic function and of students' educational experience.

Organizational culture shapes everyday reality in unappreciated, and often surprising ways; the important lesson is that strengthening institutions at the "ground level," the classroom experience, almost certainly requires interventions not usually imagined. Otherwise, academic rigor and integrity may be given up slowly, incrementally, negotiated away—dying the death of a thousand accommodations and ten thousand good intentions. The best hope for rethinking, and maybe for reinventing community colleges, consists in the effort to understand the distinctive academic culture of open access. Partly that is a matter of countless informal classroom treaties, but there is another story as well, about why the academic drift was permitted, or encouraged, and, even now, not often noticed.

2

THE REMEDIALIZATION
OF THE COMMUNITY COLLEGE

Histories are stories we tell one another. With them we try to understand ourselves, to sustain our traditions and institutions, sometimes to raise doubts and disappointment, to urge new direction. History is written many times, from different points of view, with different plotlines and different meanings.

The movement for democratic education also has not a single history, but many. The most familiar "insider" history tells the heroic tale of the triumph of open access. Other versions highlight the ironies of history. For them, the most important plot device is the unnoticed motivation, or unintended consequence—"cooling out," for instance. Usually such alternative histories coexist peacefully, since they emphasize and try to explain different features of the evolution of educational institutions (Brint and Karabel, 1989; Cohen and Brawer, 1982). Only in times of crisis will an institution be forced to choose among its histories, to discover or rediscover a guiding myth.

So our own history of community colleges is only one among many that might be written. What it tries to make sense of is less the formal and quantitative features of open access than its qualitative, experiential, and cultural features. Our plot finds rigorous academic practice moving from the center to the periphery at community colleges. Replacing it at the cultural center, encouraged by institutional arrangements, and progressively legitimated in the theories and the rhetoric of community college pioneers, are pale remedial practices—which is why we call our story "the remedialization of the community college."

37

The Decline of the Transfer Function

During their early years community colleges thought of themselves more as colleges than they do now; "university parallel" programs were much more central in their youthful self-definition. From the 1900s through the 1950s such programs accounted for 60 to 70 percent of total enrollment, and transfer rates routinely served as a critical measure of institutional success (Eells, 1931; Medsker, 1960; Lombardi, 1979). Nor was success hard to find. In a famous study, Knoell and Medsker followed 7000 community college students who transferred in 1960 to a variety of four-year institutions in ten states. Within three years of transferring 62 percent of those students received bachelor degrees; and the researchers confidently predicted that at least 75 percent ultimately would graduate (Knoell and Medsker, 1965).

Since three-quarters of all entering students typically declared an intent to transfer, Knoell and Medsker's research seemed to certify that the community college mission of access could be realized without danger of eroding academic standards. Community college graduation rates compared favorably with those of most traditional four-year colleges—even when the large community college commitment to career education was factored in. The place of the rapidly growing community college as an integral part of higher education appeared secure: local high school graduates could be provided with the first two years of college work at low financial cost and, apparently, at no academic cost. That idea has proven remarkably durable. Even in those places where the transfer function has virtually collapsed, it remains a prominent part of the story colleges tell themselves and their students. It recalls a time when community colleges in fact as well as in word promoted smooth movement between high school and university.

During community colleges' "junior college" phase, university parallel programs were the exemplary programs, in relation to which other curricular areas defined themselves. The present formal curricular and departmental organization of colleges are relics of that time when the transfer program was clearly distinguished from career, technical, and remedial programs. Similarly, if informally, the laments about declining standards also draw sustenance from the memory of when the rigorous academic practices of university lower-division courses were the models of excellence. When teachers look back, they recall, or seem to, a time when classes were taught differently, or students were better. But what these common memories really signal is just that the liberal arts university parallel program once occupied a more important cultural position than now.

The initial success of the transfer function was attained with the most traditional population of students community colleges have yet seen. Subsequently, transfer rates dipped precipitously, even to single digits in some areas. Although no well-developed national data base on the transfer process exists, the information that is available is enough to suggest the magnitude of the problem. Arthur Cohen and Florence Brawer estimate that fewer than five percent of full and part-time community college students transfer with junior status to four-year institutions (Cohen and Brawer, 1982); Kintzer and Wattenbarger found declining transfer rates in six of the nine states with large community college systems (1985). The decline has been most pronounced for minority students. Since more than forty percent of all black college students and more than fifty percent of all Hispanic college students are enrolled in community colleges, this represents a very important decline in real opportunity for those groups (Wilson and Melendez, 1984:10).

The traditional university parallel program is no longer the primary transfer vehicle. Occupational and technical programs issue more than half of all community college degrees, and significant numbers of students from those programs transfer to four-year institutions (AACJC, 1979). Community colleges no longer assume that career program students are less likely to transfer than those enrolled in liberal arts courses; almost any vocational program may now represent itself as satisfactory preparation for transfer.

This greatly complicates the problem of the academic culture of community colleges, because it makes it more difficult to decide what sorts of academic practices ought to be expected in any particular program. At the most mundane level, research on the transfer problem shows that students from terminal career programs, what were once the most important contrast to transfer programs, may actually transfer at rates higher than university parallel students. More significantly, students' apparent preference for career programs that are also transfer programs strongly implies that recovery of the transfer function cannot take the form of strengthening liberal arts sequences in the university parallel curriculum. So many "transfer students" are now in career programs that it is now hard to miss what was always the case: a successful transfer function depends less on what specific courses students take than on the strength of the classroom, on the closeness of the fit between the academic culture of the community college and that of the university.

Success with the early cohorts of relatively traditional transfer students encouraged colleges along a path from which they have never wandered. On both sides of the transfer relation, community college and university faculty and administrators came to conceive an appropriate transfer track as one that duplicates the university curriculum—what is called "articulation." Community college transfer curricula once were "university parallel." They attempted to reproduce the university lower-division curriculum with students who really were not much different from university students. Over time "university parallel" shaded into the somewhat weaker "articulation," in which the central concern is with course matching between institutions. The virtue of these was that they provided direct, formal measures for transfer courses and programs. So, even when nontraditional students began crowding community college classrooms, curricula could remain formally parallel and courses articulated—whatever the educational reality might be. Thus was transferability of courses retained even while transferability of students became a national crisis.

Fascination with articulation makes it extremely difficult to raise important questions about the nature of the preparation that community colleges offer to transfer students. Whether the dominant aspect of a transfer program was to approximate or duplicate the university lower-division, or to prepare students, by whatever means, to undertake upper-division work was a matter never really debated, never really thought open to debate. The traditional way was assumed to be the correct way—even for nontraditional students. Perhaps the road not taken, that excellent preparation may not be "parallel" preparation, deserves a second look, but the widespread decline of the transfer function has not elicited such a reexamination.

Formal course comparability remains what everybody looks for in a transfer program; "articulation" is the criterion by which they are evaluated by students, faculty, and counselors at both the community college and the receiving institution, and by registration and admissions officers at both institutions. Whatever the substantive reality may be, the more a transfer curriculum is just like (or is said to be just like, or maybe just aspires to be just like) what is offered, or is said to be offered, in the first two years at the local university, the more highly it will be regarded by everyone.

The profusion of qualifiers suggests how deeply problematic that really is and has always been. Articulation agreements based on comparability of course content can't penetrate very deeply; surely they are too weak a device, are the wrong sort of device, for ensuring the fit between the academic cultures of community college and university. Even if the long-suppressed question of whether it is a good idea for students to be doing the same sorts of things at both institutions, that courses should be in that sense equivalent, should be taken as settled, formal course articulation can't be the mechanism for accomplishing it.

Formal equivalencies, decided through the proxy of course descriptions, hide more than they reveal. They cannot specify what really goes on in the classroom—behind the same syllabus may lurk rigorous or anemic practices, strong or weak expectations, traditional pedagogy or the most striking innovation. By ignoring those critical aspects of the academic culture, by not being able to notice them, articulation agreements provide the structural framework within which the cognitive level of the academic culture can spin downward.

Faculty know that the relations between formal representations of courses and programs, say as they appear in college catalogs but also in course outlines, reading lists and syllabi, and what actually goes on in the classroom are frequently, and perhaps usually, of the most tenuous sort. Only the most rigidly structured disciplines, mathematics being the best example with the hard sciences following, are exceptions to this principle and they not always. The more common pattern is for individual faculty members, whether led by personal eccentricity, by strenuous efforts to improve students' success, or by outcome of classroom negotiation, to modify courses so that they gradually come to bear little resemblance to the official catalogue descriptions. Stipulating course comparability in the face of that natural movement—something state departments of education, or legislatures, will occasionally try—is bound to be a somewhat surreal and arbitrary exercise that unfortunately masks substantive diversity and cultural *disarticulation* in the name of a formal articulation.

As community colleges follow the logic of articulation, they mimic features of "equivalent" university courses. The opening for innovation on the academic side of the transfer problem is small; consequently, efforts to strengthen the transfer function typically treat it from either an administrative or student services perspective, with solutions proposed as one would expect for problems so framed.

For administrators, the transfer problem looks like a matter of maintaining the formal integrity of community college courses and programs within the higher education hierarchy. Formally negotiated articulation agreements are the favored device for achieving that, and are still frequent enough to be thought the rule. But problems in some regions have been so severe as to prompt bureaucratic and even legislative interventions. Florida has gone the furthest, by legislating a statewide system of common course numbering and common transcripts for all public community colleges and universities. Several other states, including California, have reinforced articulation agreements by establishing central offices to facilitate cooperation among institutions. Multicampus systems sometimes establish a central office to coordinate and facilitate transfer; for instance, CUNY assists in coordinating articulation among senior institutions and community colleges in the system (Donovan, 1987).

Formal institutional efforts to smooth transfer rarely influence classroom and curricular activities. In fact, they don't even try. They are designed to protect and legitimate current courses and programs rather than change them. Any problems about transfer are conceived as falling not on teaching faculty, but on the student service staff, particularly counselors. Student service professionals are not primarily academics. They are carriers of a social service ethos which drives them to think about the transfer problem in terms of either the social and psychological needs of students or their inability to cut through the bureaucratic thicket of higher education. Students lack information about financial aid, application deadlines, or course articulation; they are fearful and need support; they experience "transfer shock"; they have too many family and job responsibilities.

Those concerns have given rise to a wide range of student services. Many institutions have established transfer offices and have designated transfer information officers to advise students and to assist with articulation problems. Some schools coordinate counseling and advising with area high schools and major four-year receiving institutions in order to improve continuity of service. Laney College, for instance, works with counselors from the Oakland Public School District and the University of California system. South Mountain Community College cooperates with Arizona State University in a comprehensive orientation program. Miami-Dade Community College has been the leader in utilizing computerized information systems to improve student advisement with its Advisement Graduation Information System; many institutions now routinely provide microcomputer access to transfer information for their counseling staffs (Donovan, 1987).

Administrative efforts to ensure the transferability of courses, and student service initiatives to supplement academics with enriched counseling and advising—these surely count as energy well-expended, although not unqualifiedly so. They play strongly to the ways that students conceive their own transfer process (primarily in terms of their not "losing" credits), as well as to the advertising and mythology of community colleges, (primarily that community colleges offer the "same education" but at bargain rates). Certainly, it is astonishing that the weakening of the transfer function, which originally served to establish the academic legitimacy of the community college, has so often met with student service interventions, rather than with attempts to reinvigorate academics. The redefinition of relations between community colleges and universities in administrative and student service terms has been an important mechanism by which university parallel programs were displaced and the difficult educational issues about the academic role of community colleges forced underground.

This was permitted to happen because a different problem commanded the attention of the community college. By the 1970s many of the nontraditional students who entered through open doors were "underprepared." Nobody really understood how these students might be incorporated into the traditional academic culture; so the academic culture itself was changed. Theorists worked to develop new conceptions of education for these students, conceptions which were often opposed to those of university parallel programs.

In *Fostering Minority Access and Achievement in Higher Education* (1987), Richardson and Bender describe the displacement of the university parallel curriculum in this way: "the preoccupation with remediating from 60 percent to 90 percent of their entering students, along with the need to provide social services, and with the need to prepare their clientele for immediate employment, leaves [community colleges] with little energy and few resources to offer challenging transfer programs to those who enrolled with the ultimate intent of earning a baccalaureate degree" (1987:3). In their view, colleges neglected transfer programs while focusing on more pressing matters. Actually, what may have started as neglect ultimately became a matter of principle. Colleges began self-consciously to devalue traditional academics as they evolve from junior colleges to comprehensive community colleges. More and more being a "teaching institution" came to mean being a remedial institution.

The Evolution of the Remedial Function

The era of open access saw the construction of hundreds of new two-year institutions and state systems—nontraditional institutions for nontraditional students. As large numbers of academically underprepared students began to fill their classrooms, community colleges struggled to redefine their mission and articulate it to other educators, state agencies, and legislators. The distinctive language of remediation that developed decisively affected the ways colleges talk about their students, and about themselves—what they are as institutions, their societal mission, and their role within the higher education system. However, that is something best seen in retrospect; early on, few of the now familiar categories of remediation were available and certainly none of the programs.

As with the comprehensive high school, what "inclusion" has always implied for the community college is the proliferation of functions and services. Community colleges had to balance very different roles: transfer, remediation, vocational training, and community service. Each of these embodies different conceptions of the social and educational mission of the community college. As in the earlier "great school debates," waves of theory, criticism, and counterargument served as symbolic politics in which arguments about pedagogical practice held place for suppressed issues about the role of schooling in influencing poverty and the class structure.

For colleges to develop the characteristic remedial strategies, they first had to shake themselves loose from what was then the conventional wisdom, "compensatory education." That notion was introduced into educational discourse following World War II and had gained substantial legitimacy when the Elementary and Secondary Education Act of 1965 authorized billions of dollars to encourage schools to focus on underprepared, "culturally deprived" low-income and minority children. If children of the poor were to perform at levels comparable to middle-class children, schools would have to find ways to "make up for the debilitating consequences of discrimination and poverty," to compensate for the cultural deprivation of a home environment which did not support education (Chazen, 1973:35). Compensatory education regarded children's sociocultural experience as cumulative, and consequently favored early interventions such as Get Set and Head Start. Nevertheless, in the inner cities compensatory, "motivational" programs sometimes appeared as late as high school.

Despite very visible achievements, compensatory education was criticized both from the educational left and right, and made little headway in higher education. While the charge of "cultural imperialism" from the left would eventually contribute to the shattering of the decades-old consensus concerning the value of public education, from the perspective of colleges the criticism from the right was more pressing.

Compensatory programs seemed to threaten colleges' traditional sense of mission. By defining the educational problem in terms of the social and cultural experience of students, they redefined schools as social or community action agencies, rather than as educational institutions. In contrast, remediation offered neutral scientific and technological categories in place of controversial cultural or political ones. As the language itself suggests, remediation works on a medical model: specific weaknesses are diagnosed, appropriate treatments prescribed, and the learner/patient evaluated to determine the effects of treatment (Clowes, 1982:4). By concentrating on specific academic "deficiencies" of individual students, rather than on large social inequities, remediation nestled comfortably within the traditional education/social mission. By committing to remediation over compensatory education, community colleges avoided the troubling issue of cultural disarticulation, which compensatory education had at least noticed, in favor of the more manageable and ideologically comforting idea that nontraditional students lacked discrete mechanical "skills" which might be improved through application of an appropriate educational technology.

Although institutions rushed to redefine themselves by reference to remediation for underprepared students, by the early 1970s important lines of criticism were already well-established. One line of criticism raised social and cultural issues again in a new way, and questioned whether community colleges really functioned to maintain inequalities of social class. For the first time the claims of access were challenged by concerns about opportunity. Whatever else community colleges do, they also helped isolate traditional colleges and universities from the growing numbers of nontraditional students. Jencks and Riesman first noticed this, arguing that the new community colleges "are a safety valve releasing pressures that might otherwise disrupt the dominant system. They contain these pressures and allow the universities to go their own way without having the full consequences of excluding the dull-witted or uninterested majority." From this somewhat grim view of things they concluded: ". . . We doubt that the community college movement will lead to significant innovations in academic theory or practice" (1968:491-492).

"Safety valve" imagery became common coin among other critics who argued that the excessively vocational and anti-intellectual academic culture of community colleges severely limits student opportunity. Students are "cooled out," their expectations and aspirations subtly lowered by colleges which channel them away from the university parallel programs that might ultimately affect their class position, into lower-status vocational programs that reproduce it (Karabel, 1972; Brint and Karabel, 1989). Similarly, Steven Zwerling argued that community colleges "have become just one more barrier put between the poor and the disenfranchised and a decent and respectable stake in the social system which they seek" (1976:xvii). Their function is to "assist in channeling young people to essentially the same relative position in the social structure that their parents occupy" (1976:33).

Zwerling and Karabel each commented on the heavily vocational emphasis of community colleges, as compared to four-year institutions, noticing that, under the guise of providing social and economic mobility, the powerful vocational thrust of the curriculum and career counseling of students actually functions to inhibit class mobility by directing students into lower-level technical and paraprofessional jobs. The expansion of occupational education was "an ingenious way of providing large numbers of students with access to schooling without disturbing the shape of the social structure" (Zwerling, 1976:61). Despite the emphasis on remediation and the development of low-level technical skills, in fact *because* of it, community colleges were not really at the service of true democratic education. They had taken on the worst characteristics of the industrial plant and the junior high school, with a curriculum and an academic climate that prepared students only for low-level, dull, and routine jobs.

These critics raised disturbing questions about the nature of the new community college, but had little impact on curriculum and pedagogy. Partly, this was because of the hostility engendered among community college educators by outside critics who professedly rejected much of the ideology and rhetoric of "access" and "opportunity." Further, it was hard to see how to bring such analyses to bear on the administrative structures and classroom practices of the schools. Zwerling sketched one sort of class sensitive pedagogy and Ira Shor's *Critical Teaching and Everyday Life* proposed a variant of Paolo Freire's "pedagogy of the oppressed" for urban community college classrooms, but these were far out of the mainstream (Zwerling, 1976; Shor, 1980; 1986). The most important of the first-generation community college theorists had already opted for scientific and technological solutions to the problem of nontraditional education, conceiving it in cognitive psychological rather than in sociocultural terms.

That much more widespread style of analysis, which we call "the educational effectiveness criticism," argued that traditional college curriculum and pedagogy could not be effective with the mass of underprepared new students. But whereas left critics took that failure to be a matter of public policy, educational effectiveness critics took it as a technical challenge. Advocates of this approach believed that community colleges could reconstruct their curricula, student services, and pedagogy to make an inviting and supportive environment for nontraditional students. Success could be elicited even from students with a long history of failure.

The educational effectiveness critics conceded the relation of higher education to class structure, but tried to soften that issue in several ways. K. Patricia Cross, for instance, disputed the left's assumptions about what the "new student" population really looked like. In *Beyond the Open Door* she described these students as "new" to higher education because only in an age of open admissions would they be considered "college material"; they ranked in the lowest third of high school graduates. Cross disputed the easy identification of nontraditional or underprepared students with racial minorities. She argued that most actually are drawn from the white working class, even the middle class: "two-thirds are first-generation college students . . . over one-half are white, about 25 percent are black, and about 15 percent other minorities . . . The majority of high school graduates ranking in the lowest academic third are white" (1976:6).

Further, Cross contended that it is illegitimate for public policy to shift the meaning of education equality from individual to group mobility. Arthur Cohen and Florence Brawer also explicitly-offered a liberal response to the social goals of the left critics, arguing that no form of schooling can "break down class distinctions ... or move entire ethnic groups from one social stratum to another" (1982:353). In this way, they tried to release community colleges from direct reliance on any particular social or political agenda. Community colleges were to be ideologically neutral, concerned only to enhance educational opportunity to broader segments of the population.

But when the educational effectiveness critics examined what colleges were actually doing with underprepared students they found conventional and mostly ineffective programs. Students whose previous academic performance was marginal or failing were encountering either regular college course work for which they were clearly not ready, or replays of what they had already failed at. Remediation helped those on the borderline of acceptable academic performance; but, as Cross remarked, "We have not found any magic key to equality of educational opportunity through remediation" (1976:9). Remedial efforts operated on the fringes of higher education, in what were only partly legitimate vestibule programs, and had not penetrated into the instructional core of colleges.

In John Rouche's first national study of remedial programs, he found only limited commitment to remediation. Reviewing programs in the late 1960s, he noted that, "as many as 90 percent of all students assigned or advised into remedial programs never completed them ... little wonder that critics of community colleges soon referred to the open-door policy as a 'revolving door policy' " (1968:48). Most remedial programs consisted mainly of watered-down versions of regular college-level courses, housed within regular academic departments and taught by faculty with little preparation and little commitment to remediation. Rouche and Cross both applauded the comprehensive programs that were developed in the 1970s as distinct improvements on that picture. The new programs offered a broad range of educational services and teaching strategies, had a volunteer teaching and counseling staff, and were often housed within separate divisions of remedial education (Rouche, 1973). They offered a glimpse of the coming "instructional revolution" needed for colleges to be educationally effective. In Cross's sanguine assessment remediation "started as a simple approach to equality through lowering the access barriers ... turned into an educational revolution involving all of higher education. The revolution has reached the heart of the educational enterprise—the instructional process itself" (1976:9).

According to its advocates, the instructional revolution would be based on "mastery learning," individualization of instruction, and new learning technologies. Starting with remedial programs, where the sense of crisis was acute, the revolution in pedagogy was imagined as spreading throughout community colleges, and then to the other sectors of higher education. Community colleges were to be the distinctive vanguard institutions of the instructional revolution. Their large commitment to the difficult project of remediation would force them to innovation, and their success would encourage others to follow. Change of this magnitude would call for ruthless single-mindedness. Familiar classroom practices such as lectures and group discussions probably would be replaced in the great effort to enhance student achievement. As Arthur Cohen put it: "[given the] aim of engendering minimum, fundamental achievement in all students . . . all the instructional processes are then directed toward bringing students to this goal" (1969:22).

For improved educational practice these theorists drew from cognitive psychology, which seemed to them to suggest that instruction ought to be radically individualized. Things like programmed and computer-assisted learning, with their emphasis on self-pacing, active participation, clear and explicit goals, small lesson units, and frequent feedback, were especially recommended. These practices would enable even students with a prior history of failure to achieve success by leading them through carefully graduated learning sequences, from the simple to the complex, the speed of movement and difficulty of task always geared to the present capabilities of each student.

The "educational effectiveness"; theorists—Cross, Rouche, Cohen, Brawer—saw themselves as encouraging community colleges to become "achievement-oriented" institutions. Following the precepts of the instructional revolution, at last community colleges could offer a realistic promise of educational achievement to the vast majority of their students. They spoke from within the great tradition of Progressive education which attempted to develop a science of instruction and to place it at the service of incrementalist social reconstruction. However, with the emergence of so-called developmental programs in the 1970s, community colleges turned away from the path projected by the Progressives. They were torn by competing impulses, by alternative visions of the precise nature of their mission with underprepared students.

The Developmental Drift

The educational effectiveness movement was the work of theorists and policymakers; what came to be called "developmental education" was more the diffuse creation of a multitude of active classroom instructors whose experience disposed them away from educational technologies, and more generally, away from primarily cognitive understandings of remediation. Developmental educators argued that the familiar remedial concern of bringing students "up to college level" in their "basic skills" was only part, and maybe not the most important part, of what the community college ought to be doing for the students that were overflowing the remedial classrooms.

Advocates of developmental education did not define themselves in the tradition of Progressive education, with its model of cognitive psychology informing an ever improved practice. Instead, they portrayed the goal of their efforts in terms of the ideal of a fully developed, multifaceted self that successfully integrates the cognitive and the affective aspects of personality. Frequently, developmental educators looked to the psychological theories of Jerome Bruner and Jean Piaget for support. From them they drew the notion of developmental stages, of readiness to acquire concepts and skills. From the humanistic psychology of Carl Rogers and Abraham Maslow they took an emphasis on the importance of empathetic communication in promoting personal growth, the need for teachers to fully accept student individuality and nurture it. The vocabulary of remediation began to look cold and unfeeling. The talk of "educational technology," "intentional learning," and "the teacher researcher" was rejected at the ground level in favor of notions like "developing the whole person," and "helping students understand themselves and their lives."

The shift from remediation to developmental education happened quietly, without rancor or debate. Since they rely on such utterly different accounts of college mission, of proper classroom goals and methods, perhaps that is surprising. Indeed, often each explicitly defined itself against the other, portraying itself as trying to accomplish different ends by different means and for different reasons. More often, however, the two camps talked past each other, and, in any case, lacked any institutional means to articulate and settle their differences. What finally happened was that the alternatives merged institutionally, and appeared to merge theoretically. Developmental goals—developing personal con-

sciousness, changing affective styles, encouraging social competence, enriching the lives of students, their families, and their
communities—were no longer clearly distinguished from the remedial goals of ameliorating skill deficiencies. In the 1970s and
1980s programs began to describe themselves as "remedial/devel-
opmental," and pursue a peculiar blend of cognitive and personal
development goals.

Remedial categories continue to guide admissions testing and
placement, and entrance and exit criteria for precollege courses.
Those are all described in terms of the mastery of writing, reading, and computational skills; and, of course, precollege programs
are dominated by reading, writing, and mathematics courses. Developmental understandings deeply shape the way faculty actually
teach those courses, however, and what they value about them.
When teachers share stories, they are less often about how students have increased their academics skills, than about how "one
of my students now reads to her children," or how another "registered to vote for the first time." Teachers in developmental programs are extremely concerned with issues of students' self-
esteem, their personal growth, and feelings of autonomy;
counseling is a critical element in those programs. As one observer
notes: "Counseling is considered almost a panacea in that it is
supposed to give high-risk students the extra attention they need"
(Moore, 1981:20).

The affinity between developmental programs and the student service function commonly results in institutional alliances
between developmental faculty and counseling staff. Richardson
and Bender notice that since the counselors have an ambiguous
relation to the academic function, those alliances are not entirely
benign. "On the negative side, the existence of a special cadre of
staff [student services] who see themselves as protectors of the
open-door philosophy for the underprepared has produced fewer
academic solutions than desirable . . . the rift between academic
and student service staffs . . . can erupt into conflicts that stymie
efforts to deal with the issues of academic quality and standards"
(1987:49). Counselors often oppose the imposition of academic
standards; according to Richardson and Bender, they think of
themselves as student advocates. As the cryptocounseling stance
of developmental instruction established itself throughout the
community college, the counseling staff was tremendously reinforced by an energetic and committed developmental teaching faculty. Since they were now trusted colleagues rather than wary

adversaries, long-standing, latent tensions between academics and student services became even more deeply submerged. Both jobs, it appeared, could be accomplished without compromise.

The confusion of function of remedial/developmental programs accelerated the weakening of the academic culture of the community college. The new programs lacked the clarity of vision of either the purely remedial or purely developmental, although they appropriated much of the vocabulary and many of the practices of each. The important point is that in remedial/developmental programs cognitive and affective achievement are not clearly distinguished, and are actually allowed to drift together.

Inevitably, the mixing of the "hard" outcomes proposed by remediation, with the softer ones of developmental programs, made the hybrid "medial/developmental" programs notoriously difficult to evaluate. The fact that few students ever successfully made the transition from the special precollege programs into the regular curriculum was not taken to show those programs to be failures; instead, such programs could be defended as encouraging and facilitating the full mental, moral, and emotional growth of students whose lives might be enriched by their coming to know, to appreciate, and ultimately to express themselves fully as members of society and as members of their social and racial group. If the universally dismal outcomes of precollege programs no longer produce a sense a crisis, it is because developmental "social service" goals have eclipsed the traditional cognitive objectives of higher education.

The broad processes by which community colleges have been remedialized are clear enough although the particulars of the story differ from state to state and even from college to college. Carried by and proselytized by a committed faculty, remedial/developmental understandings and practices spread from precollege programs both vertically and horizontally, even into university parallel programs. That process is encouraged by institutional practices that effectively scatter underprepared students every where. Academic policies may reduce core course requirements and restrict prerequisites. Admissions, testing, and registration policies may produce somewhat haphazard placement. Funding formulas and financial aid policies often encourage rapid movement from precollege programs into regular college courses, or concurrent placement in them. And, of course, counseling and advising almost always puts very high value on maximizing student choice. Of those common policies some are freely chosen, others are forced on institutions. Taken individually, and certainly in combination, they result in extreme heterogeneity of the classroom: almost any student may be registered in almost any course.

In the era of open access, even declared transfer-oriented students look underprepared to faculty, and are in fact drawn from the lower quintiles of the public high schools. They are considered college level only because so many of their fellow students are even less well-prepared. When the illiterate, the somewhat literate, and the literate, sit side by side in the community college classroom, the distinction between remedial and "regular" students, and between the remedial/ developmental function and the traditional academic function, will be blurred or even obliterated. A very vigorous academic culture, constituted by the social and intellectual practices of the academic disciplines, might have resisted these powerful tendencies. However, at community colleges, unlike universities, academic disciplines have only a very weak status— for example there are no upper-division courses, and often few sophomore level courses. Disciplines might have relied on university conceptions of academic rigor, but when transfer relations with universities were finally interpreted in terms of the bureaucratic concern of articulation, community college courses were cut loose to follow their natural paths. As it turned out that path was away from discipline-specific concerns and toward generic conceptions of instruction.

From remediation and the educational effectiveness movement, faculty took a vocabulary for describing underpreparedness. Some prescriptions they found congenial, such as careful sequencing, and breaking complex ideas into simple elements; but they stopped short of adopting the full range of educational technology. The also began to use the vocabulary and exemplary practices of developmental programs. The result of this dual movement was the reshaping of the typical classroom, and more globally, of the entire academic culture. What came to predominate was a mixture of a mechanical "skills" activities, and information retrieval— which taken together are what Richardson calls bitting—with a social service mission of individual affective development.

Pedagogy and Ideology

What is troubling about the remedialization of community colleges is the extent to which it seems to reinforce the left's critique of community colleges, that under the banner of providing enhanced educational opportunities they unintentionally help perpetuate the dual structure of American education which works to deny meaningful social mobility. What becomes of students is largely a matter of how their education shapes them; that in turn depends on what settings and practices they encounter and engage. The history we have sketched has seen the weakening of both faculty and student expectation about what counts as rigorous academic work. Intellectual activity became debased and trivialized, reduced to skills, information, or personal expression—for students who look to education as their chief hope of advancement. The remedial and developmental practices that now largely constitute the academic culture of community colleges are far too weak to elicit the powerful transformations needed to really make a difference in students' prospects.

We have earlier argued that nontraditional education is best thought of in terms of cultural disarticulation. This provides a novel way to understand the precise nature of the two-tiered structure of American education. Of course the "two tiers" reflect and help sustain the racial and class divisions of American society. Partly, they are able to do this because they are very different cultural enterprises, striving through their practice to form students in particular ways. Ironically, the educational practices offered to children of professionals at four-year colleges and universities are tougher, more rigorous, and denser than those offered to the nontraditional students for whom education means the most.

Notice, for instance, the very different status of language in the academic programs, and the lives, of more traditional students at more traditional sorts of schools.[1] For them, reading and writing is not a matter of mastering semantic, syntactic, and orthographic correctness, as in remedial programs. Nor is it a matter of students being provided with unfettered opportunities for intellectual, aesthetic, moral growth, and "finding their own voices," as in developmental programs. For traditional students, academic reading and writing is part of a style of life that is rich and meaningful beyond the classroom. Academics is for them a system of progressive initiation into various communities of discourse. Similarly, in community-based literacy programs students' progress with language and thought is usually firmly anchored in what are real world problems, dilemmas, and possibilities (Kozol, 1985).

Not so for remedial or developmental students. For them language and thought are rules to be mastered, so divorced from any meaningful use that one of the great concerns among their teach-

ers is how to find or create appropriate adult materials at grade
school levels. Semesters, possibly years, of what has to seem to
them to be drudgery will precede any useful and significant outcomes for them. If traditional students had to engage in countless,
essentially pointless exercises before their real engagement with
academics could begin, their retention rates might begin to approximate those of remedial students and far fewer bachelor's degrees would be awarded.

The developmental solution to the debilitating apathy associated with dictionary exercises and mechanical drills is to embed
skills instruction within various genres of personal expression.
Thus, little reaction papers, opinion papers, journals, and personal
narratives—thought to be intrinsically rewarding as well as educationally worthwhile—have mostly supplanted repetitious mechanical drills. Both, however, are in striking contrasts to the sorts
of cognitive and expressive activities that characterize traditional
classrooms, and which constitute the cultural core of the academic
and professional world. To put it bluntly, weak academic practices
subtly exclude nontraditional students from that world, rather
than inviting them into it.

None of the ideological accounts of the mission of the community college, a list of which practically retells their history, ac-
knowledges the full dimensions of the educational challenge of
nontraditionality, of the problem of declining intellectual or literacy standards. Since neither educational practices nor proposed
outcomes are independent of ideology, or of each other, major pedagogical alternatives have to be thought of as much more significant than the happenstance choice of individual classroom
teachers. They are devices by which society molds itself into a certain image. For liberals, educational practices should promote individual achievement in a competitive setting that is conceived as
essentially meritocratic; the nontraditionality of students is to be
addressed by large social service organizations within the collegiate structure. Vocationalists interpret pedagogy as training—
rote memorization, the mastering of a myriad of tasks, and
preparation for a specific and delimited role within a rigid professional hierarchy. The social activist tries to counter the "hidden
injuries of class" by bringing students to full consciousness as
members of an oppressed group so as to promote collective political action to alter the existing social and political arrangements.
The triumphant remedial and developmental attempts to reconstruct community colleges draw variously on those familiar com-

peting ideologies, in the sort of eclectic appropriation that ought to signal failure rather than success. But none of the reigning ideologies recognizes the cultural features of nontraditionality. None encourages rigorous intellectual work for nontraditional students. Apparently, powerful intellectual training is to continue to be reserved for an elite; for the second tier, language competencies will be the mechanical, the informational, and the expressive.

If nontraditional students are to be adequately prepared for academic success, there must be substantial transformations in their conception of education and their sense of themselves as learners. Correlatively, nontraditional institutions have to change in ways that allow nontraditional students to experience education as something more than simply memorizing, reciting, expressing, and opining. If this has been hard for colleges to see, it is because pale intellectual practices haven't been entirely accidental. They have been endorsed as reasonable and beneficent, as implied by cutting-edge educational theory, as offering nontraditional students the best environment for academic success. The relation between the academic culture of community colleges and the standard educational theory which supports it is so tight that any substantial reform of practice will require a reform of theory.

3

DISORDER IN THE CURRICULUM

In higher education, what is called reform almost always turns out to be incremental adjustment, rearranging the furniture, trying again what didn't work ten years ago. That is natural enough. People are used to thinking about problems in familiar ways, and entertaining a familiar range of solutions. Any culture constrains change, primarily through the apparent self-evidence of shared assumptions. Those mostly remain hidden and insulated from debate; the usual conversations are all that are usually possible. Reform ambles along accustomed paths.

Although community colleges like to portray themselves as curricular and pedagogical revolutionaries, they are actually quite conservative. They have remained firmly committed to an educational wisdom which interprets reform and innovation narrowly. Conventional innovations—learning packages, individualized instruction, computer-assisted learning, and developmental education—do not run counter to institutional culture; they are live options within it. Even those relatively easy sorts of reform can encounter rough going: turf to be defended, budgets to be fought over, intransigent faculty and administrators to be persuaded. Reforming the academic culture, however, will not call for large capital expenditures, nor grand political accommodations; it faces a problem of another kind. Since it is sure to challenge or ignore the conventional wisdom about education, it will seem not just wrong but wrongheaded. Nothing can be done about that except confronting it directly, by recalling to consciousness the assumptions by which educational institutions swear.

The Canonical Model

The prevailing wisdom about curriculum and teaching is less than a century old. What is now the ordinary way institutions think about themselves originated in the exciting Progressive vision of effective public schools set at the service of democratic education. It has suffered the fate of much reform: what begins as animating vision ends as workaday routine. Routinization has long ago stripped away its status as optional and problematic theory; now it seems natural and transparent. Almost everyone thinks it to be so obvious that any deviation is bought dearly. We call it "the canonical model."

On the canonical account, the curriculum is the institutional plan for moving students from their beginning profiles, through a series of experiences and activities to a specific endpoint. It is the rational pursuit of consciously chosen ends. The process of curriculum construction, of converting goals into reality, is clear-cut and often even mechanical. First, curriculum planners identify the outcomes to be achieved. The goal statements they formulate are then precisely operationalized into sequenced behavioral objectives. Appropriate teaching methods are chosen for achieving each objective. Finally, evaluation instruments are designed to measure student progress. As the curriculum is put in place the central issues shift to supervision and evaluation. Administrators continually oversee and review the entire process to ensure that objectives are met.

This "Tyler rationale" of curriculum development and pedagogy—stating objectives, selecting learning experiences, organizing those experiences, and evaluating them—was extremely influential in the public schools (Tyler, 1950). From there it travelled to community colleges, introduced by first-generation administrators who had begun their careers in the high schools. The image of curriculum as the product of thoughtful and responsible deliberation has proven remarkably appealing. Especially attractive was the proposal that the educational process could be guided by a scientific understanding of the relation between goals and the methods for achieving them. Appropriate roles for both faculty and administrators can be neatly mapped onto that distinction between ends and means—the definition of outcomes, the responsibility of administrators, the selection of instructional processes, the province of faculty judgment.

Once this was doctrine to rally behind, its origins revolutionary; now its power derives mostly from simple habit and lassitude. Once it drove the great educational reforms which produced the familiar institutional forms of American education; what remains are the whispers or echoes of those great debates. The various allies and opponents had argued from within different traditions, but found common ground on two important issues. The first was the universal call for a science of educational practice to replace the religious, moralistic, and ineffective traditional education. On this point, Progressives, most notably John Dewey, joined with men such as Edward L. Thorndike and John B. Watson who were seeking to put psychology on a more scientific footing. "Scientific psychology" was to be at the service of educational reform. Carefully crafted experimentation would discover "the laws of learning" needed to guide a revised pedagogy (Powell, 1965; Robarts, 1968; Eisner, 1979). This effort to scientifically ground teaching converged with the attempt by other educational leaders to reform school management by appropriation of the new industrial scientific management techniques of Frederick W. Taylor.[1]

In the beginning decades of this century, education was heavily influenced by the "cult of efficiency." As early as 1911 the NEA appointed a Committee on the Economy of Time in Education, charged to determine the applicability to education of the new scientific management (Callahan, 1962; Dorst and Sneeden, 1967). Frederick Taylor had recently revolutionized management theory and practice, advocating an empirical, experimental approach to workshop supervision. He argued that traditional haphazard industrial organization adversely affected production. Achieving maximum productivity meant rethinking and reordering industrial tasks into the demonstrably most efficient mode of performance, the uniquely best organization of work. The standard examples of the success of the principles of scientific management were the new time and motion studies, which systematically analyzed complex operations into simple movements. Unnecessary movements were eliminated; the entire work process speeded-up, reconstructed, "rationalized." Autonomy of individual workers was rejected as inefficient; instead, management would mandate a standard method and time for each task. "In the past," Taylor declared, "the man has been first; in the future the system must be first" (quoted in Hughes, 1989:188).

Taylorism, the belief that the scientific method could discover the laws of behavior governing industrial organizations, decisively altered the relations between management and workers. The scientific reconstruction of the workplace in the interest of maximizing productivity was a historic break from the tradition of the craftsman. It created a radical separation between the planning and performance of work. Rather than encouraging or even permitting workers to seek solutions independently for problems on the shop floor, management would train them in the one best, most "rational" way to perform their tasks.

Taylor was a leader in the vanguard of American culture which looked to set engineering to the job of social reconstruction. The same principles of industrial engineering that had pushed America into economic prosperity soon resonated outside the industrial plant, now going under the rubric of "social engineering." Distinctions among engineering, management, and other human activities eroded. The historian Thomas Hughes puts it this way:

> Inventors, industrial scientists, engineers, and system builders have been the makers of modern America. The values of order, system, and control that they embedded in machines, devices, processes, and systems have become the values of modern technological culture. . . . Their numerous and enthusiastic supporters from many levels of society believed their methods and values applicable and beneficial when applied to such other realms of social activity as politics, business, architecture, and art (1989:4–5).

Franklin Bobbitt and W. W. Charters urged schools to follow the example of industry as transformed by Taylorism; education should focus exclusively on its "product" and the detailed processes for creating it. As educators "learn to adapt the newly developed job specification, scales of measurement and standards of attainment . . . we shall have for the first time a scientific curriculum for education worthy of our age of science" (Bobbitt, 1913:49). That sort of ideological fervor was very important but it underplays an important element in the appeal of scientific management. When craftsmanship was supplanted by efficiency in industry, and later when the teaching environment began to be compared to the shop floor, the guiding imperative was the need for exponential increase in the level of production. The best way to produce education on the same massive scale as electric lighting or automobiles would be to refigure schools along the lines of industrial plants. Only a rationally engineered educational production system could produce the large numbers of graduates demanded by the advocates of democratic education (Bobbitt 1918:42).

Educational institutions took from Taylor's industrial scheme its strict separation of planning and execution in the workplace. Responsibility for goal setting and quality control went to managers, "administrators"; teachers would merely carry out their assigned tasks within the overall instructional plan. Thus began the long process of the deprofessionalization of teaching.

Contemporary organizational theory strongly rejects the image of organizations as social machines and managers as social engineers. In its place, theoreticians now favor imagery of family and community. On this new account, managers should be less concerned with "top down" directing, and more with consensus building, and with enhancing worker loyalty and commitment to customer satisfaction. But the organizational structures and management styles formed at the beginning of the century linger (Peters and Waterman, 1983). At educational institutions also the structures, conceptions, and categories of the canonical model continue to shape debate and deliberation. The language of education has become opaque to the people using it; its social history and controversial theoretical assumptions are ignored or forgotten.

Scientific psychology and scientific management were invoked by educational reformers not because they were neutral to educational debate but because they necessarily pushed debate in particular directions. As novel theory passed into conventional wisdom, its strongly partisan nature was forgotten. That tacit account of what learning is and how it is achieved, what educational institutions are for and how they are to be reformed, has slipped from consciousness—as if being embodied in our institutional structures, being lived, it need no longer be thought.

The Problem with the Canonical Model

The conventional educational wisdom depends on deeply problematic assumptions about the nature of knowledge and cognition, about learning, and about the nature of human action. Those assumptions are of relatively recent origin, having been taken from scientific management, early scientific cognitive psychology, and empiricist epistemology. More recent theory has completely superseded those earlier orientations, to the point that no direct counterargument is any longer needed. In any case, the problem with the canonical model is not really that it is wrong, but that it constrains thought, and forces it down certain narrow paths. Consequently, it hides the social and cultural features of educational institutions, and reinterprets them on its own terms. The weakening of the academic culture of community colleges, and the problem of nontraditionality, are each made invisible, or to look like other problems, with other solutions. Later we will propose a new language for describing the academic culture of community colleges, but first it is worth noticing how the ordinary language of education misdescribes it. We will focus on two assumptions: 1) that curricula are best conceived instrumentally; 2) that curricula should be mapped onto cognitive psychology.

1. The Curriculum as Instrument. The canonical model portrays administrators and teachers as fully rational actors, carefully planning and choosing, in control of their institutions, shaping them to their will. Curricula and teaching strategies are the instruments they work with to achieve the goals they have for their students.

This is an excessively purposive account of institutional activity which claims much greater direct control over processes and outcomes than is possible for an educational organization, or any organization (Georgiou, 1973; Weick, 1982). When institutions elude control, when reform fails, for example, a manager who thinks of himself as a social engineer will enjoin larger, more detailed interventions. However, by interpreting the social and cultural dimensions of schools as if they were freely and purposefully chosen means to ends, the canonical model ignores or masks the most basic ways that the behavior of teachers and students is actually shaped. Cultural practices are seriously distorted when thought of as the neutral instruments by which teachers and administrators achieve their goals. As contemporary organizational theorists constantly reiterate, guiding institutional change requires a more nuanced appreciation of cultural dynamics than is available within any instrumental theory.

Thinking of the curriculum and teaching strategies as instruments suggests that they are culturally neutral, but they're not. The favored interventions within the canonical model—things like careful coordination of instructional means with administrative ends by means of "learning objectives," or the widespread adoption of educational technology—do not operate on the academic or institutional culture from the outside. The infusion of such practices and the suppression of traditional pedagogies create a new academic culture; they do not simply add on to the old one.

One of the peculiarities of the canonical model is that although it sees curriculum as an instrument, and relies on cognitive psychology to develop a science of instruction, nevertheless it has not followed Taylorism in opting for a unique best process of teaching to be imposed throughout the schools. Instead it has come actually to encourage extreme eclecticism of practice. The theoretical reason for this is that curricular theory and cognitive psychology both look to an epistemology in which knowledge is only loosely related to methods of inquiry or learning. Consequently knowledge may always be arrived at, or learning accomplished through various routes.

Community colleges have been behind no one in developing alternative strategies to accommodate diverse "learning styles." If anything is now dogma at community colleges, it is that a thousand flowers ought to bloom, that no single teaching technique is the best one, and that different students respond to different processes. Diversity is harmless, even beneficial, we are told, since "we're really all after the same thing." That sounds nice enough but hardly anyone notices that it implies the detachment of disciplinary content from distinctive disciplinary practice. The degradation of the academic culture of community colleges has been partly achieved in that way, by repackaging disciplinary cultures as generic skills and information. The resulting ideology of neutral eclecticism may now be the biggest obstacle to meaningful curricular reform.

2. Cognitive Psychology as a Guide for Curriculum. To create a science of instruction, early curriculum theorists turned to scientific psychology, specifically cognitive psychology.[2] This has not been entirely beneficial. Translating the sociocultural enterprise of education into cognitive psychological terms distorts practices at all levels, but at open-access colleges, with their large population of adult nontraditional students, the issue is critical.

Cognitive psychology never really shook free from early empiricist imagery which pictured learning as experience writing on blank slates, and hence on analogy with how children learn. From Piaget, Vygotsky, and Perry educators took stage developmental accounts that modeled education on maturation; intellectual development was taken to be movement from relative deprivation to the acquisition of repertoire. Because of the natural scientific framework which supports it, the maturational line is thought invariant; thus what might otherwise be though cultural differences in cognitive styles and performance are translated into relative success and failure in normal development. Nontraditionality become deficiency, the failure, for instance, to acquire linguistic and computational skills in a timely fashion. In a science of instruction informed by cognitive psychology, learners are undeveloped, childlike. While that may be fine when students actually are children, it certainly is not with adult nontraditional students. They are not blank slates upon which faculty may write.

Since cognitive psychology developed as a species of individual psychology, it dissolves the social and cultural dimensions of education into aggregates of individual behavior. Classrooms and colleges look like teachers, one by one, interacting with students, one by one. Consider the following discussion from a well-received book about college teaching:

> Even a relatively simple analysis of an educational task may be useful. For example, one might ask, "why does a student fail an essay question on an exam?"
>
> 1. She does not understand the question.
> 2. She has not learned the material.
> 3. She lacks cues for retrieval.
> 4. She lacks an appropriated strategy for retrieving the material.
> 5. She lacks words needed for an answer.
> 6. She lacks a conception of the required solution; for example, when asked to 'explain,' she lacks an adequate conception of what is involved in an adequate explanation.
> 7. She cannot hold the required material in active memory while writing the answer (McKeachie, 1978:235).

From the perspective of learning theory, that just about covers it. However, the attempt at exhaustiveness is revealing; notice how completely the scene is painted as an isolated student failing a particular question because of various deficiencies, "lacks." Usually she lacks information, sometimes cognitive strategies. A familiar road is being travelled here: when failure is construed as inadequate retrieval or strategy, success drifts toward becomes information and skills acquisition—bitting.

Remarkably absent from the list of putative explanations are both other students and the teacher; whatever the problem is, it's inside the individual student's head. That the students as a group might carry cultural styles or modes of thinking resistant to the preferred styles advanced by the teacher—nothing like that is entertained. Students are not pictured as having any prior cognitive commitments, as having already been shaped in ways that affect how they confront the teacher and the material. They are quite pliable and plastic, perhaps even a bit childlike, since a child's learning problem may very well be a lack of information, skills, or strategies. But adult education is more like reshaping and restyling than filling an empty bucket, or writing on a blank slate; more like a transformation than initial formation.

Curricula driven by cognitive psychology tend naturally to innovate in the direction of individualized instruction. When cognitive styles are explained by invoking neurology and biology, rather than sociology and anthropology, students will be thought best served by isolation from an academic culture rather than by immersion into it. This very seriously miscasts the relation between higher levels of cognition and the social and cultural organizations which cultivate them and give them meaning.

For example, in his famous study, William Perry offered a scheme of cognitive development for the college years. Initially, students are "dualists." They see issues in binary terms, as right or wrong; they recognize and accede to scholarly and teacherly authority. From there they should progress to relativism, the stage during which they challenge authority, and more generally, reject all claims to truth as ultimately unsupportable. If all goes well they eventually make a "commitment within relativism," thus reaching Perry's highest stage (1970). However, although these were offered as cognitive psychological stages, they are actually more illuminating as "cognitive anthropological" stages. The action is not primarily inside the student's head; the different stages describe her changing social position within the academic community. Students arriving from authority-structured high schools naturally enough operate as dualists. Their exploratory, lower-division college experience shapes them toward relativism. As upper-division majors they will have to explicitly embrace disciplinary norms and practices. Seeing students' changing cognitive styles within a primarily psychological framework misses all that, and so misses the extent to which education is a social act.

Colleges are not social machines producing educational products, nor are teachers and administrators social engineers. Curricula are not neutral instruments for producing changes in students, nor are schools staffed by fully self-conscious and rational actors. By offering such a picture, the canonical model misdescribes the central social and cultural features of community colleges.

The Intellectual Hidden Curriculum

So great is the multiplicity of function of community colleges, and so great the eclecticism and diversity, that they can hardly be intelligibly described as single institutions at all. "This college is really many colleges," one often hears. Put another way, the most striking cultural feature of community colleges is that they lack a center; they are not driven by any unitary view of what education, especially nontraditional education, is all about. As new institutions they had no strong traditions to draw on. Since the canonical model encouraged them to regard curriculum and pedagogy as purely instrumental, they took from here and there, theory from this and that tradition, practices from wherever.

Canonical educational theory sees pedagogical practices and curricular content as the conscious design of faculty and administrators. Consequently it offers a vocabulary of efficiency in understanding schools, their failings to be traced to ineffective coordination of instructional means and ends. For interpretive social science that all looks like the wrong cast of characters. Since schools are cultural sites, and curricula cultural artifacts, what is really needed is an alternative vocabulary of commitment, practice, and tradition for understanding what are more like public symbols and rituals than products of rational calculation.

When schools are understood as cultural artifacts the conscious purposes and choices of the staff will seem less important. What moves into focus is the language of the participants and the social practice to which it gives meaning. Curricula become the public space where the informal, latent theoretical commitments of faculty members, departments, and divisions meet and interact. Often, as we saw in the case of the remedial/developmental accommodation, very different, even opposed, educational traditions can coexist peacefully—or seem to.

The academic culture of community colleges is not so much ineffective as unintelligible. Because of their distinctive history, open-access institutions are incredibly complex cultural settings characterized by a diversity of pedagogical practices through which faculty unconsciously play out differing and sometimes conflicting educational commitments.

This is a pattern familiar to cultural historians. For instance, in *Habits of the Heart* Robert Bellah and his associates argue that American culture comprises several different languages of self and society (1985). Although Americans primarily speak a language of "individualism," they find its categories too limited to capture the complexity of personal and political commitment. When people wish to understand the personal relationships and the public involvements that matter most to them, they switch to the "second languages" of America. All these languages can be traced to different roots. The language of individualism comes to us from eighteenth century liberalism. The second languages harken to more ancient origins: the classical republican and Biblical traditions. These languages and the traditions and theories they express exist only in uneasy relations with one another in this century.

Similarly, in his extremely influential study, *After Virtue* (1981), Alasdair MacIntyre argues that modern public life has the aspect of a debate among half-forgotten theories. Participants talk past one another, using largely misunderstood fragments of vocabularies that have been severed from their relations with history and practice. From the inside theoretical diversity seems fundamental, and incoherence ineluctable. Only the purported expertise of scientists, engineers, and scientific managers claim exemption from thoroughgoing relativism. People who fail to appreciate the historical contours of the problem try to settle matters by the imposition of some favored theory, proposed as canonical, but that just lends one more voice to the confusion. Competing cultural traditions and practices do not simply disappear on request. All this produces a tangle of theory and practice that cannot be understood along any single dimension or within any one theoretical perspective.

The intellectual history developed in *After Virtue* and *Habits of the Heart* suggests how the complex academic culture of community colleges might be reconstructed and displayed. Certainly educational practice feels disordered, in disarray—if the frequency of calls for reform is any measure. Surely educational debate is burdened with multiple incommensurable vocabularies of description and justification. Working ourselves free from the sense of incoherence and futility calls for a kind of cognitive therapy which recovers and reorders what has been forgotten. So, following Mac-Intyre and Bellah, we trace how the language and practice of open access relate to submerged theoretical commitments.

To help sort through the relations between particular educational theories and particular pedagogical practices, we introduce a novel piece of terminology: "educational agenda." With it we analyze the varied ways education is pictured or enacted in particular pedagogies, and assumed in the vocabularies that faculties use to explain and justify what they do. The apparatus of agendas is useful for making explicit what is usually overlooked, hidden.

One way to understand the agendas is in terms of what a perfectly self-conscious and rational person would recommend as practice in the light of particular theoretical commitments. Of course, nobody ever has those mythical perfectly self-conscious and rational people to cross-examine. Very much to the contrary, faculty are prisoners of received vocabularies, reshaped under the pressure of daily performance; so no educational agenda could be taken as a fully adequate description of any individual teacher or classroom. Agendas range over practices and the theories to which they give embodiment. We recognize that in ordinary usage "agenda" denotes the conscious plans of particular persons, but that is not intended here. Agendas constitute the intellectual hidden curriculum of a college; they are implied by and carried by practices; only very infrequently do faculty fully recognize or articulate them.

The Skills Agenda. The deepest penetration of the skills agenda has been in the remedial programs whose steady growth and tremendous influence has ensured that curricular debate can never be unaffected by its terms, nor any program entirely insulated from its practices. The very familiar idea is that the level of students' basic skills has plummeted so far that colleges should directly pursue the goal of skills enhancement. Of course the notion of "skills" is vague enough to allow purveyors of different wares to treat it as institutional common coin. However, its distinctive force is that complex and sophisticated achievements, "higher-level skills," rest on, and may even be analyzable into simpler discrete achievements, "lower-level skills."

Although the vocabulary of skills is used very freely, the core notion itself is fairly precise. Acquiring a skill means learning how to do something well or correctly. More pointedly, one speaks of skills in contexts that are rule-governed, contexts in which what is at issue is whether rules have been followed correctly or incorrectly, whether results are right or wrong. At lower levels, say in remedial programs, "correctness" or "rightness" is conceived orthographically, syntactically, or computationally; the hoped for achievements are correct speech, or writing, or computation. At higher levels what counts is correct argumentation, or analysis. Pedagogy associated with "skills" instruction relies very heavily on repetition and practice, "drill," work with "problems," and memorization of rules.

Teachers working within a skills agenda mine educational psychology, especially cognitive developmental theory. Piaget and Vygotsky are most frequently appealed to, and routinely paired as holding that each developmental stage lays the necessary foundation for the next one. The interpretation of literacy as skills, the conception of skills as arranged on a logical hierarchy, and the mapping of the logical hierarchy onto the temporal sequence of biological development—this is taken to imply that the teaching of writing, for instance, must recapitulate the stages of functional development. Apparently, if in a child the cognitive structures of stage A precede those of stage B then that ought to be the sequence of teaching, even for adults.

Cognitive psychologists differ sharply on the issue of the "plasticity of the mind." But for classroom teachers, insulated from those disputes, there is tremendous appeal in the notion that basic linguistic and computational skills can be mapped onto developmental stages, more appeal still in the common sense view that those skills must be learned in pretty much the same way and the same order as the teachers themselves learned them, or remember learning them.

A skills model of intellectual activity subtly imposes much of the apparatus of the canonical model. For example, it invokes the familiar sharp distinctions between "skills" and "content," between "method" and "findings." On that grid, courses are of two basic sorts: those that teach *how* to think, or read, or write, or compute (skills courses), and those that provide information, that teach *what* to think (content courses). When that conceptual division has been made the big question that teachers dispute is whether skills and content are necessarily intertwined, or whether they might be taught effectively in isolation from each other.

Remedial programs, with their emphasis on correct orthography, syntax, and computational mathematics are natural homes of the skills agenda. But even more sophisticated intellectual activities

are often thought of as just "complex" skills, somehow built out of
the simple, lower-level skills. In higher-level courses, such as
"Critical Thinking" classes, the activities may be mostly rule-
following, and evaluation a matter of whether the rules were followed correctly. Learning the rules of logic or argumentation by
practice with informal fallacies on logical puzzles is the same kind
of activity and the same modeling of the mind as applying the
rules of grammar, or using algorithms in arithmetic to achieve
correct results. Writing and computation beyond the remedial
level are on a skill model if they are "broken down into simple
steps" the correct performance of which constitutes acceptable
writing or problem solving. When the highest level cognitive
achievements are described as "analysis" and "synthesis"—the
breaking into logical parts and the putting together into an integrative and summative whole—the metaphors guiding practice
will inevitably be mechanical rather than organic or cultural.
Thus a pedagogy of repetition, drill, and memorization will intrude, if not predominate, wherever intellectual activity is conceived as algorithmically rule-governed.

The Cultural Literacy Agenda.   The skills agenda works
one side of the canonical skills/content dichotomy; the cultural literacy agenda works the other. Its contrast and complementarity
with the skills agenda is quite striking: where the skills agenda is
concerned with "correct" and "incorrect" rule-following, cultural
literacy is interested in information, the "true" and "false." Teaching and evaluative strategies stress the acquisition and retrieval
of information: lectures, textbooks, and multiple-choice examinations, for example.

The cultural literacy agenda has been widespread in American public education since its beginning. For about as long, reformers have been pointing to its central practices as what is really
wrong, what really needs reform. The peculiar twist in recent educational debate has been the theoretical resuscitation of cultural
literacy. Now it is being proposed as more than what teachers like
to do, but as the most important goal of public education.

In his best-seller *Cultural Literacy,* E. D. Hirsch advances the
neoconservative view that education is primarily a device for holding together a fragile social order (1987). The social integrative
fuction of education, he claims, requires mass inculcation of a common authoritative repertoire. Hirsch's own argument has been

couched in appealing terms, as the attempt to revive the flagging democratic potential of education. Whatever students' skill level, he argues, if they fail to master the "canon" they are forever outsiders, blocked from meaningful participation in the intellectual, civic, cultural, and professional life of the community. For Hirsch, the repertoire turns out to be "information," "knowledge," that all educated people know. This resonates strongly for many community college teachers, who experience daily the cultural disarticulation of their students in those terms, and complain that students cannot recognize the most casual allusions to history, art, books, plays, even movies. Cultural literacy encourages them toward developing courses which "expose" students to the humanities, the social sciences, the arts, and the sciences.

Where the practices of cultural literacy are most prominent, academic disciplines are presented in an entirely confident and authoritative mode. "Common information" loses the tentativeness that disciplinary practitioners assume, and is treated instead as "knowledge," as facts about the world. Similarly, high-level theories seem like transparent lenses for seeing the world directly. Functional sociology becomes sociology and analytic philosophy becomes philosophy in classrooms dominated by information exchange and retrieval. When the student's educational task is to "tell me what I told you," crucial issues of theoretical and interpretive perspective are set aside, perhaps never to return.

That may not always be bad. After all, particular disciplines command different cultural positions. The natural sciences are extremely self-assured about their ability to decide what's true; the social sciences somewhat less so. Naturally, they are likely to think that the initiation of new students requires them to master basic information. In contrast, the knowledge claims of the humanities are so attenuated that those disciplines have sought for almost a hundred years to carve out a niche on the skills and values side of the standard dichotomies rather than on the fact or content side. The humanities have been so devalued relative to the sciences that they often abandon epistemic claims entirely, and justify their content by explicit appeal to a social integration function. In general, where claims to truth are strongest, pedagogies that depend heavily upon memorization are most common and evaluation typically conducted by "objective examination." Where the claims to truth grow weaker the vocabulary of "opinion" begins to intrude and, inevitably, "subjective examination."

The Critical Literacy Agenda.   Cultural literacy represents learning as knowledge acquisition through memorization of facts; however it is seldom found standing alone. The language and practice of critical literacy derive from the belief that students should be invited to higher-order achievements: not only do they need knowledge but also the ability to acquire more knowledge, and to assess competing claims to knowledge. This is accomplished by the students operating within standard theoretical networks, using their respective categories, vocabularies, and methods, and applying them to novel situations. To the extent that information transfer is involved in that, pedagogical practices will be those of cultural literacy: lectures, textbooks, the use of authoritative sources, and objective examination. However, more distinctive critical literacy activities try to make students junior practitioners within disciplines, to bring them to think and talk, to understand in ways characteristic of a particular theoretical perspective, as behaviorists, for instance. Lectures shade into lecture/discussions; term papers, laboratory reports, and essay examinations become favored devices.

Practices of critical literacy are not as widespread as those of skills or cultural literacy. Because of the remedialization of the community college, the latter are extremely prominent, and together constitute the cognitive orientation of most precollege courses, and many college level academic courses as well. What is interesting about critical literacy is that it is so often purported to be the highest level achievement for students.[3] Perhaps this is because it attempts a synthesis of the skills/content dichotomy, and consequently looks like the enriching of the other agendas. In the practices of cultural literacy, disciplines are pictured as informational networks. But they have another side as well. Ordinary practitioners recognize that they are governed by constraints analogous to correct application of skills—the obvious example being the "steps to be followed" in the "scientific method." In terms made famous by Thomas Kuhn, critical literacy tilts toward "normal science," and the training of the "normal" scientists who work on the day-to-day puzzles and projects falling within the range of a theory which remains for them unproblematic (Kuhn, 1970). For students this presents itself as the call to think creatively within standard theoretical frameworks, as well as memorizing the firmly established detail, and mastering ordinary laboratory skills.

Disciplines such as mathematics, physics, and chemistry occupy cultural positions so powerful that they speak to students with entirely authoritative voices. With varying degrees of success other sciences and technologies ape the posture of the natural sciences, appeal to them for support, and explicitly look to mold themselves in their image. As we argued earlier, educational theory joined in the rush to reform itself as a "science of instruction"—the effort that produced the canonical model of curriculum. The skills, cultural literacy, and critical literacy agendas seem to form a total educational package because each picks up one piece from the old canonical categories. Together they exhaust the categories and notions of method that were culled from the nineteenth century image of science, and formalized in the twentieth century under the rubric of "empiricism."

None of that enjoys the scholarly consensus it once did; contemporary theorists emphasize historical, cultural, and interpretive studies over the more traditional natural science models. But earlier efforts to displace simplistic empiricism went about it differently, by drawing on metaphors of artistic creation.

The Personal Development Agenda. Although not spread widely through the curriculum this agenda is particularly important in the humanities, and through the humanities strongly influences conceptions of literacy and practices of writing instruction.[4] Its advocates may explicitly try to counter other agendas, complaining that they are too narrowly focused on information acquisition and scientific forms of cognition. In their view, education should be more concerned with nurturing students' personal, moral, and social growth, with the cultivation of their unique identities. They prefer practices such as expressive or creative writing, private journals, ungraded writing, freewheeling discussions, and generally activities which seek to elicit "insight," and cultivate a natural, "authentic voice." In developmental education programs, which are heavily staffed with humanities faculty, the personal development agenda encourages cocurricular activities designed to enhance the self-esteem and the racial or ethnic pride of students—putting on little plays, for instance, or digging into "roots," poetry readings, meetings with community activists, and so on.

The personal development agenda primarily uses language and metaphors drawn from the Romantic tradition. Nineteenth century romanticism had self-consciously offered itself as an alternative to the Enlightenment, as challenger to its empirical and representational account of knowledge and cognition. Specifically, Romantic theorists believed that modern science illegitimately displaced the human mind from the natural world through its acceptance of the "subject/object" distinction captured so well in the image of the scientist studying alien inert matter. The artist was to dislodge the scientist as cultural hero; a vocabulary of "creation" and "expression" would replace "representation" and "scientific method."

Romantic theorists fully intended a complete reorientation of how cognition was conceived.[5] They offered metaphors of action to supersede the traditional metaphors of sight. Consequently, knowledge was described as a creative act of consciousness valid only for a particular person or group rather than an objective correspondence between "propositions" and "facts." The whole bestiary of traditional epistemic objects—knowledge, perception, fact, theory—were redescribed: invented rather than discovered, evolving or growing rather than accumulating, expressions of the self rather than objective features of the world.

The tension between the two languages, or even that there are two, goes unnoticed because empiricism claims to explain artistic creation and subsume artistic categories. Generally, cultural activities at some distance from natural science, such as art and aesthetics, but also religion, ethics, and even politics, get reduced to noncognitive sentiment or "values" which are explainable by sociology or psychology (MacIntyre, 1981; Schwartz, 1986).

As a matter of history the Romantic attempt to usurp the central cultural position of the natural sciences failed. However the languages of empiricism and romanticism remain strong alternatives.

The Interpretive Literacy Agenda.   One of the great challenges to the hegemony of positivism and empiricism came from the Romantics, with their elevation of the artist to exemplary figure and the process of artistic creation to the model of a fully lived human life. The other great challenge came from within science and philosophy themselves. The nineteenth century saw the rapid development of cultural disciplines which relied on interpretive practices and literary categories, and consequently emphasized the historical boundedness of cognition. Even "scientific," "analytic," or "objective" thinking was cast as ineluctably rhetorical. At its higher levels it is marked by the ability to unravel and display embedded or implicit argumentative and explanatory structures, to position them relative to one another, and to find ways to adjudicate among them. The empiricist imagery of the isolated independent mind confronting an essentially inert natural world with only "experience" and "method" as guides, was replaced by the metaphor of knowledge as conversation, shaped by and expressed within historically constituted communities.

One way to understand what is at issue between empiricism and its romantic and interpretive opponents is to see how a traditional model of intellectual life, say, Socrates, appears to each. Empiricism draws on a much older tradition that thought Socrates interesting because of how he stood against his community and criticized it. His greatness lay in his developing an ahistorically valid method for independently and objectively judging moral and practical issues. From this Socrates flowed the philosophical Platonism that saw knowledge as inner illumination, and philosophers—later scientists—as teachers with special access to Truth.

When Romantics revised traditional views of Socrates what they most noticed was Socrates' life rather than his method. They admired him for expressing a new form of life, for creating by force of his distinctive character, his inner *daimon,* the life of philosophy that was subsequently twisted in unfortunate ways by his pupil, Plato. Socrates' frequent denials of special knowledge strike them as more persuasive than the later imputation to him of Platonism, and consequently they emphasize his injunction that it is the form of life that counts, the reflective or "examined" life that is worth living.

For the interpretive or hermeneutical tradition Socrates is the greatest of the Sophists. What it notices about him is not how he stood over and against his community, but how deeply embedded in that community he really was. The life he engaged in was not drawn *ex nihil* from his inner soul; the moral figure of the teacher and Sophist was familiar. Nor were the debates he joined timeless controversies; they were central to the public life of his time. His great achievement was the reshaping of Athenian tradition, his distinctive contribution the reflective articulation of the ideals of his community. For the interpretive tradition, what the case of Socrates reveals is the extent anyone is tied to his discourse community and the extent he may wander afield.

For the interpretive tradition all cognition and knowledge is dialogic, and rooted in the practical concerns of a particular time and place. Learning also is conceived dialogically, rather than mechanically, more a matter of learning how to engage the community on its own terms than the acquisition of information. Consequently, pedagogy stresses the use of primary texts, especially ambiguous or problematic texts. Whereas the cultural literacy agenda treats texts as exemplars of standard positions, for the interpretive agenda the real issue is finding or generating perspectives or metalanguages in which they might be understood more deeply and sympathetically. Even so-called canonical texts are treated as rhetorical specimens: situated within a "network of discourse," and requiring subtle and intricate unraveling, contextualizing, and "deconstructing." Familiar activities such as classroom discussions take a characteristic dialectical form, tacking explicitly from the object level to the formal metalevel, from talk about society, for instance, to talk about the talk. Writing assignments depart from the familiar genres, "description," "exposition," "persuasion," to become what Kinneavey calls "dialectical" or "exploratory" (Kinneavey, 1980).

In the last quarter century the most important contemporary currents of thought have joined in the critique and rejection of the empiricist conception of knowledge and learning. The interpretive agenda consequently has regained prominence. However, community colleges have been almost entirely insulated from "postpositivistic" or "postfoundational" styles of thought.[6]

*   *   *

Which of the intellectual agendas, or what mix, dominates in any particular course depends partly on the outcome of classroom negotiations, partly on teacher inclination. But it is influenced in important ways by the cultural status of the various disciplines. The uncertain status of the humanities, for example, makes them especially open to confusion of agenda. Philosophy provides a particularly striking example. Philosophy's claim to cognitive authority has so weakened that courses will sometimes tilt toward the teaching of "argumentative skills" (the skills agenda), sometimes toward teaching a repertoire of information about the great philosophers or about "perennial problems" (cultural literacy), sometimes as training within currently favored styles of philosophical argumentation (critical literacy), and occasionally toward developing "personal philosophies" or "values" (the personal development agenda).

The status of history is also interesting. Sometimes it presents itself as deploying a distinctive social scientific method, perhaps quantitative social history. Often it hitches its wagon to a Hirschean star, and offers itself as the repository of cultural literacy. But, not uncommonly, it adopts a humanistic pose, and describes its own activities as artistic or interpretive.

Because of the central cultural position of the natural sciences, other disciplines define themselves in relation to them. For example, since psychology is closely allied to the natural sciences, especially biology, it is strongly physiological and even reductionistic. Very likely it will be taught within a cultural and critical literacy framework: a standard authoritative textbook surveying the field from an unproblematic perspective. In contrast, social psychology is more likely to be pursued interpretively. Not nearly so self-assured, more deeply concerned about what counts as its methods and objects of study, it is consequently more inclined to portray itself as in search of them and so to return to classical texts (as opposed to textbooks).

Outside the traditional liberal arts, practices and commitments cannot be captured along purely cognitive dimensions. Community colleges have long been committed to a vocational function: preparing students for careers. But even there mixed intellectual agendas underlie and sustain pedagogical practices. Career education programs include activities which shape the style and affect of students as potential workers in ways similar to those in which the cognitive agenda shapes students minds. But these are not entirely independent matters. To the extent that vocational programs picture the professional and paraprofessional worlds they will be parasitic upon the cognitive agendas: low-level, mechanical, and repetitious careers mapped onto skills; the paraprofessional mapped onto critical literacy; and professional, responsible, innovative careers onto the interpretive model.

The Confusion of Agenda

When the problem of the academic culture is noticed at all, it is usually described in terms of the "levelling down" or erosion of academic standards and practices. However, our discussion of the various educational agendas reveals complexity that is missed in that sort of framework, and missed by faculty who do not look beyond their own particular courses to the academic culture they collectively create. The real problem of the academic culture of open access is not weak theory and practice but disordered theory and practice. Consequently, academic life as experienced by nontraditional students cannot be other than severely disordered and unintelligible.

Imagine a typical student's academic experience—not any particular classroom but the shape of the whole. The curriculum, and perhaps even individual courses, will be a mix of pedagogical practices that draw on different understandings of disciplinary and intellectual activity. In sum, they attempt the impossible: simultaneously to educate students according to radically different conceptions. Put bluntly, there is no sustained effort by the faculty to collegially shape students' cognitive styles, to form their minds. Sometimes the practices call for rule-following of a mechanical sort, sometimes remembering facts, sometimes expressing feelings unconstrained by rules, and sometimes working within particular theories. Since curricula are organized primarily on a disciplinary basis, all of this remains in the background, the "hidden curriculum," that acts more certainly and powerfully than the official curriculum.

Uncoordinated and unacknowledged, the intellectual hidden curriculum is sure to seem mysterious to nontraditional students, for whom the disorder and confusion of agenda means the absence of an academic culture. They cannot but ultimately decide that academic life has no unity beyond the idiosyncratic requests of individual teachers. For many that is what mass secondary education has predisposed them to believe anyway, that their real task is impressions management, their real goal grades.

The criticism and discrediting of the theoretical apparatus upon which canonical educational theory rests has not yet had apprecible impact anywhere in education, certainly not in high schools or community colleges which are relatively detached from the world of scholarly debate. Still, the lineaments of reconceived educational practices suggested by the new scholarship are striking enough, and encouraging. New categories of analysis, patterns of curricular thought, and styles of pedagogical practice are all implied by the move from educational thought modeled on the physical sciences and technology, to educational thought drawn from the human sciences and cultural studies. Those offer images of initiation and conversation as ways to understand knowledge and culture and, of course, education. For an educational system deeply involved with serving a nontraditional population, where the tacit assumptions about the cultural match between students and faculty have broken down, the offer is too tempting to be refused.

The nontraditionality of community college students is not really a matter of their slates being blank, of their having "lacks" or deficiencies which faculty must remediate, of their being more or less passive objects upon which educational technologies might operate. Students striving to enter the academic and professional communities, not fully understanding the nature of those communities, certainly not displaying the intellectual and affective styles and practices which constitute them—such students need to be invited and enticed to join and to stay. It is a mistake to think of that as reimposing rigor. Nor can it be a matter of simply requiring more general education or liberal arts courses, or dissolving the culture of colleges into students' interactions with computer terminals.

The difficulty with the last of these perhaps is clear enough. Most contemporary curricular or pedagogical reform travels down the other road; so it is worth now changing the level of abstraction to talk directly about such efforts.

4

THE LURE OF GENERAL EDUCATION

At universities the nationwide procession of general education reforms has engendered a robust skepticism among faculty and administrators. Nevertheless, at community colleges the least mention of general education reform usually has the same effect as ringing the bell at the beginning of a prize fight. Faculty glimpse the cultural dimension of the problem of the nontraditional student, although they usually cast it in terms of students' motivations, attitudes, and generic abilities. Intuitively, they turn to the area of the curriculum which historically has claimed concern with forming the minds and hearts of students, with shaping their characters. So while the battles over general education sometimes seem fruitless and trivial, they are really about the most pressing problems of democratic education.

General education may be concerned with very important issues but, given its history, it may be a singularly poor device for reinvigorating academics at community colleges.

The Ambiguous University Heritage

The history of general education reform is complicated: its contemporary versions echo the earliest disputes over what the proper formation of students should be and which academic practices should stand as exemplary. The tale tells of modern universities struggling with specific problems quite different from those open-access institutions face today, or will face tomorrow. Although on all accounts general education is by far the most troubled component of university curricula, here, as in many things, community colleges followed the universities, and somewhat unreflectively adopted their approaches. The university's uncertainties about the nature and purpose of general education have spread to the community college.

General education has always had a confused and ambiguous status at the university level. Consider a recent statement about what problems general education reform is supposed to address:

> The undergraduate college, the very heart of higher learning, is a troubled institution. . . . Educators are confused about how to impart shared values on which the vitality of both higher education and society depend. The disciplines have fragmented . . . and undergraduates find it difficult to see patterns in their courses and to relate what they learn to life . . . Colleges appear to be searching for meaning in a world where diversity, not commonality, is the guiding vision. (Carnegie Foundation for the Advancement of Teaching, 1986).

Notice the problems that are grouped together—the difficulty of imparting shared values, the fragmentation of the disciplines, the difficulty students experience in relating their learning to life, and the more general loss of meaning in a world where diversity rather than commonality is the rule. These are all familiar subjects for educational jeremiad. Still, the list is peculiar: how did these problems get grouped together so that the "fragmentation" of disciplines is related to a loss of meaning in "both higher education and society"? Why is it conventionally believed that those are aspects of one problem or one set of problems that might perhaps be settled at one stroke? The rough answer to these questions is that in the great university debates about general education, multiple rhetorics of social crisis and alternative visions of educational solutions gradually melded. This spawned the familiar cycle of strong rhetorical advocacy of general education followed by meager impact on student experience.

The modern conception of general education originated in the latter part of the nineteenth century, when higher education was first explicitly set to the social goal of economic growth. In particular, Charles Eliot, president of Harvard, pioneered what Laurence Veysey calls "the utilitarian vision" (Veysey, 1965:118). Eliot criticized traditional "classical" education on the grounds that it failed to offer students the specialized knowledge required for the new scientific and professional careers that were beginning to dominate in the American economy. The traditional, fixed curriculum should be replaced with a free elective system which

> would allow individual students to discover and develop their
> 'natural bent'. . . and prepare themselves freely for a place of
> their own choosing in life . . . and . . . insure an intelligent
> public opinion . . . that indispensable condition of social
> progress (Eliot, [1869] 1978:563).

The idea that college curricula should promote individual and social utility was a powerful vision of educational reform which found ready support among the new professional associations concerned with cultivating scientific and technical expertise. Eliot's views were widely discussed and stimulated important reform, most notably at the University of Wisconsin and Cornell University at the end of the nineteenth and beginning of the twentieth century.

The free elective system advocated by Eliot was a significant step in the creation of the modern American university. It encouraged greater specialization of faculty, and much greater attention to graduate and professional education (Miller, 1988:16–17). The open, diversified curriculum permitted faculty to teach their own research interests, and increasingly they did just that. Gradually the movement for utility in higher education, with its emphasis on career preparation of students, and the involvement of faculty in public issues, merged with the ideal of the research university, best represented by the model of the new Johns Hopkins (Veysey, 1965).

Even a century ago, all this did not go unchallenged. Its opponents charged that the utility movement was excessively vocational and narrowly intellectual; they argued for maintaining the central curricular role of traditional "liberal culture" (Miller, 1988:19). This movement was strongest at small liberal arts colleges, especially on the East Coast, and in those larger universities where the classical curriculum retained influence. It was concentrated in departments such as philosophy, modern languages, and literature, where the ideals of research and utility were not yet fully established.

By resisting the movement to the modern research university, advocates of liberal culture portrayed themselves as recalling colleges to their traditional mission of developing the educated gentlemen who would be responsible leaders in their local communities.

For that, the curriculum had to be directed to cultivating minds and characters, not to imparting specialized methods and information. Their vision of professionals who are deeply committed and involved in their communities contrasts sharply with the utilitarian image of the neutral professional whose role consists in objectively applying technical expertise. The new man of science was to "exchange general citizenship in society for membership in the community of the competent," but this was precisely what proponents of liberal culture rejected (Haskell, 1984:67). For them, the point of education was to build the strengths of character and mind needed for responsible judgement and civic leadership. To that end the rhetorical tradition provided better guidance than the new scientific curriculum (Proctor, 1988).

These competing concerns have guided curricular debate ever since. The utilitarian vision underlies graduate and upper-division curricula, where specialized training, the major, is what counts. Associated with it are credit distribution and free elective systems, and an emphasis on student autonomy. The legacy of the tradition of liberal culture appears primarily in lower-division curricula where concern may be more for the "whole" student, for intellectual development conceived more broadly than specialization in most academic majors allows, and for moral and civic education. The tension between these basic views of education drives much curricular reform; in particular it engenders a search for curricular unity in the face of departmental sovereignty.

The desire to balance professional specialization with republican and religious ideals of civic education has fueled general education revivals for almost a century—without resolving the underlying problem. As Boyer and Levine suggest in commenting on the general education movement of the 1920s:

> Reformers had very different notions about what the university should do and where society should go . . . Most important, general education advocates failed to recognize inherent contradictions in their thinking . . . between the demand that higher education adapt to the complexities of the modern world, and the equally insistent call to recapture the ideals and cultural unity of the prewar era (1981:12).

This deep rift in the conception of public education is not usually recognized. Publicly funded state universities, in particular, strive to achieve through the curriculum what were once thought competing goals: training in specialized disciplines and the integration of students into the civic culture. However, the modern research university is so driven by the utilitarian vision that it is unlikely to be able to realize the aims of the competing liberal culture tradition as well. The generation and transmission of specialized knowledge is only obliquely related to the kinds of things Boyer and Levine think colleges should be concerned with:

> shared values, shared responsibilities, a shared heritage, and a shared world vision . . . our common life must be reaffirmed, our common goals redefined, our common problems confronted . . . the preservation of democracy, the promoting of a common heritage, the development of citizen responsibility, a renewed commitment to ethical behavior, the enhancement of global perspectives, the integration of diverse groups into the larger society (Boyer and Levine, 1981:18).

Whether universities can simultaneously produce technically competent and publicly involved citizens is problematic. However that should turn out, the models of general education reform that have developed at universities are entirely misleading guides for community colleges. There, conversations about general education may continue in ways made familiar by a century of university debate and still ignore the fundamental educational problem of community colleges—the disarticulation of nontraditional students from the practices of academic life. This is worth seeing in more detail.

Contemporary University Models

The most common model of general education reads the solution right from the problem. If students are becoming overly specialized by concentrating in narrow disciplines, then general education can add breadth where there is already plenty of depth. Breadth components may take various forms; but the call to despecialize, within the utilitarian vision, will usually suggest a credit distribution system. Such systems attempt to "broaden" students, but without any strong commitment as to what broadening might be for or what it might compromise. For community colleges the danger in this is very real. Since the whole point of lower-division work is left open on a credit distribution model, it encourages a brew of competing agendas which undermines the academic culture.

General Education as Cultural Recovery.   During the periods of reform, alternative accounts of general education take credit distribution systems as their polemical opponent. Typically, the language of broadening is retained, but with the specification that it proceed through the creation or recreation of what has been perceived to be lost or never really had, a common culture of educated people. Currently, the most widely discussed proposal portrays general education as cultural literacy—a common fund of knowledge, ensemble of skills, competencies, and attitudes that any educated person must have.

However, if the civic culture is fragmented in the way that advocates of general education maintain, then it is extremely implausible and tendentious to cast the "generally educated" person in substantive terms. Unless some relatively narrow community is the arbiter, there simply isn't a common body of knowledge, ensemble of skills, attitudes, and competencies that commands wide assent. Were it otherwise general education would not be such a perennial topic, nor would it so often be conceived as recovery, rather than as maintenance of commonality.

College committees routinely, if half-heartedly, produce lists of characteristics of the generally educated as goals for general education courses. Their reservations express the widespread belief that those general education goals are not really achievable by very many students, that the best that can be done is to "expose" them to art, literature, and philosophy. When general education is reinterpreted downward, toward "exposure" to the liberal arts, it will have tremendous appeal. By then its lofty goals will have been reduced to what classroom teachers already do; by then it will call for minimal alteration and disruption of current practices.

Thus, teachers can continue to conduct their classes in the ways they always have, by lecturing about their areas of interest, while comfortably believing themselves engaged in the critical task of cultural recovery. The ease with which universities can slide into interpreting general education in terms of special disciplinary expertise naturally finds its most perfect expression in credit distribution systems. But it also appears, somewhat veiled, when the appeal to recover a rich cultural heritage is reduced to teaching a network of information dear to disciplinary savants.

But something more pernicious lurks in the cultural literacy account of general education. Hirsch notices the growing disarticulation between the professional culture and the civic culture, between the academy and its novices, and concludes that "traditional literate knowledge, the information, attitudes, and assumptions that literate Americans share—cultural literacy ought to be normative (Hirsch, 1987:127). The point is subtle but ought not to be missed. Seeing the general educational problem as "cultural illiteracy" implicitly imports imagery of primitiveness, impoverishment, and immaturity. Inevitably, rote memorization (perhaps of Hirsch's 65-page list of "what every literate American should know") and skills drills become the favored modes of instruction. After all, that's what we've always done with children, savages, and the culturally deprived isn't it? Hirsch sees this connection:

> Our current distaste for memorization is more pious than realistic. At an early age when their memories are most retentive, children have an almost instinctive urge to learn specific tribal traditions. At that age they seem to be fascinated by catalogues of information and are eager to master the materials that authenticate their membership in adult society (1987:30).

Hirsch, of course, is concerned only with children: openness to enculturation in his view is biologically constrained by age. For community colleges the implications would be darkly pessimistic, since presumably the game would be up by the time students reach college. But the imagery of students as children or as culturally deprived adults resonates in tune with the perfectly natural wish to idealize the dominant academic culture.

The educational problem for college students, and adults generally, is nothing like the problem of initial acculturation—so the anthropological evidence Hirsch cites about how tribes teach their children is not really to the point. Adult learners already are bearers of culture; the exchange between them and the academic community, to extend Hirsch's example, is more like the relation between different tribes than between parents and children. It calls more for a theory of cross-cultural communication than an account of personal growth toward cultural and cognitive maturity. Students coming to open-access institutions are already formed in very important ways, shaped by their immersion in prior practices. Because cultural literacy misconstrues disarticulation as deficiency, it is an inadequate and even reactionary guide for educational practice.

General Education as Common Learning. Another influential alternative to credit distribution approaches to general education was advanced by Boyer and Levine in *A Quest for Common Learning*. For them, the fragmentation of the intellectual world which has specialized curricula as its educational expression calls for holistic integration. General education "is the educational tool we reach for in our search for renewal of the frayed social compact" (1981:18). The big issue is not whether individual students are specialized or well-rounded; rather it is the role of the university in restoring a shattered culture:

> During each revival, general education spokesmen consistently have been worried about a society that appeared to be losing cohesion, splintering into countless individual atoms, each flying off in its own direction, each pursuing its own selfish ends (1981:18).

General education "reaffirms our connectedness" through study of "those experiences, relationships, and ethical concerns that are common to all of us simply by virtue of our membership in the human family at a particular moment in history" (1981:19). This analysis suggests to them interdisciplinary courses and curricula which focus directly on relations among disciplines, and on the universal features of human experience.

Much of the rhetorical power of this account depends on the subtle conflation of two very different senses of "common learning." For advocates of cultural literacy, it is "learning *that* all people have in common." Boyer and Levine also favor a unitary curriculum at the service of social cohesion, but their twist is that the knowledge everyone should share ought to be of *what* all people have in common.[1]

At elite universities, where students are thoroughly trained in particular disciplines, there may be great merit in things like "capstone" seminars which attempt to generate a "common agenda for study and investigation and a common discourse" (1981:19). And perhaps it is natural that once the path of rounding-out specialists has been chosen the common topics should "cut across disciplines."

But at community colleges the educational problem is quite different. Whether or not universities are in a position to use general education to heal the rift between disciplinary specialists and the civic culture, community colleges certainly are not. Their job is to bridge the gulf between nontraditional students and academic life. At institutions where students are struggling to join disciplinary communities, the backgrounding of disciplinary norms and practices in favor of interdisciplinary general education courses cannot have an entirely benign effect. Quite the contrary, it can be expected to weaken the academic culture further by diluting discipline-based standards of rigor and norms of discourse.

General Education at Community Colleges

Not everyone at community colleges is convinced that students should be subjected to general education requirements at all, whereas others see in general education the salvation of the community college. The surprising thing is that although that sort of debate is potentially very heated, faculty and administrators alike approach the issue of general education with the marked skepticism reserved for perennial topics: periodically discussed, cosmetically redone, dismissed. For the area of the curriculum implicitly deemed so important that all students must take it, for courses supposedly expressing the most basic value judgements of the faculty and their view of an educated person, that is perhaps startlingly cavalier treatment. The reasons for that are a bit complicated, but are mostly traceable to two sources, one that people often notice and one that receives almost no attention.

The first of these is that general education is the area of the curriculum which organizationally belongs to no one in particular, so that, as Boyer and Levine put it, "General education . . . is the easiest place to dump those concerns that everyone agrees are serious, but for which no one seems willing to take responsibility" (1981:3). The history of the various general education movements of this century is practically a catalogue of goals which simply have no other curricular home. Among those concerns have been things like moral training, global education, and social cohesion; now we are seeing it praised for its merits in overcoming academic deficiencies (Boyer and Levine, 1981:9). While one might see mere confusion in such a multiplicity of goals, the more important point is that none of the plethora of candidates for general education goals has a natural home among the academic culture of disciplines, nor any specific departments committed to their achievement. Since general education operates outside the organizational structure of disciplines, general education reform tends quickly to take on the trappings of religious revival. Particular faculty and administrators act as missionaries, attempting to fire the enthusiasm of their colleagues for activities outside the province of normal disciplinary work. Such efforts ordinarily start with a bang and whimper slowly away; energetic commitment counter to natural inclination is notoriously difficult to sustain.

This problem is even more striking at universities, which, after all, have seen many more cycles of general education reform than community colleges. Since faculty power and prestige reside in individual departments, and professional advancement is linked strongly to participation in national professional organizations and to publications in specialized journals, faculty members have had few incentives to work so far afield from the sources of their own scholarly interests and identity. Even when powerful coherent programs have been designed, faculty have been extremely reluctant to invest enough time and energy to make them successful. The classic instance of this was the Harvard University 1945 report, *General Education in a Free Society,* the so-called "Redbook" which tremendously influenced national discussion of general education but which was decisively rejected by the Harvard faculty itself in favor of pursuing general education goals through distribution requirements.

The traditional locus of faculty power at the university, the department, is much weaker at community colleges, especially in the liberal arts. The best analogue to the power wielded by university departments is in selective career programs that control both recruitment and certification of students. Where departments have power they use it; in those areas faculty display the same rather distant stance toward general education as university departments.

That general education is organizationally orphaned is often remarked upon. But it is related to another issue, less often noticed, that general education is theoretically orphaned as well. Put technically, educators treat it as a "residual category." It encompasses whatever remains after disciplinary findings and methods have been exhausted. The liberal culture movement tried to fill that residual space with particular substance, and even now the general education movement expresses a longing for the values and traditions of the nineteenth century liberal arts college.

Although originally general education was the expression of liberal culture, it need not, and indeed, has not remained limited to that specific educational vision. Since it is a residual category it can accommodate ideas taken from many places. Knowledge and methods may have been preempted by the special disciplines, but still colleges can promise "to enlighten the citizenry through general education" (Cohen and Brawer, 1987:177). The liberal arts especially may lose their disciplinary constraints and "become adisciplinary, integrated studies for people who want to understand their world and their place in it, who study concepts more directly related to civic action. Developing a sense of social responsibility is the general education ideal" (Cohen and Brawer, 1987:11). Obviously this is an echo of the liberal culture tradition, but since so little of that is retained, the specification of the residuum is bound to seem trite and unconvincing: ". . . the liberal arts should be taught in interdisciplinary fashion because students become citizens who must use integrated knowledge for answering questions arising in their own lives or in the society of which they are a part . . ." (1987:11).

Commonly, at community colleges, the call for "integrated knowledge," for study of what eludes specialized study, slides toward the suggestion that general education should be concerned with generic abilities: "principles of rationality, language, judgment, criticism, inquiry, disciplined creativity, sensitivity to cultures and the environment, and awareness of history" (Cohen and Brawer, 1987:7). Implicit in this sort of translation of the residual into the generic is the assumption that generic abilities cannot be cultivated by work in the academic disciplines.

The same merging of information, "understanding," affect, and generic skills as comprising the features of "an educated person" can be found in many of the current proponents of general education, and in the standard lists of general education goals published by many colleges. Robert H. McCabe of Miami-Dade Community College, the home of a standard model of general education at community colleges, puts it like this:

> What is most important that students do take from the college years is a better understanding of our society and others, a capacity to deal effectively with other people, a value system as the basis for decisions, competence in learning and basic-information skills—the ability to find, read, analyze, interpret, communicate, and the ability to formulate new ideas and to make decisions (McCabe, 1988:109).

Since the liberal culture tradition is even weaker at community colleges than at research universities, the concerns that first animated the general education movement are twisted in peculiar ways. For instance, the overriding concern of the liberal culture tradition was with cultivating civic responsibility. That tradition is so muted at community colleges that theorists substitute a liberal and utilitarian appeal to social order. Arthur Cohen and Florence Brawer put general education at the service of integrating poor and working class students into the dominant culture:

> The colleges—junior and senior alike—have maintained the liberal arts not only because of tradition but also because such studies are deemed basic to societal cohesion. The dominant American culture rests on literacy, shared values, common understandings, an appreciation for diverse points of view, respect for traditions. Each new generation must be acculturated . . . (Cohen and Brawer, 1987:7).

Here the problem is seen as a society in constant danger of disintegration but for the intervention of formal education. Cohesion is accomplished by acculturation; but, in their rhetoric, cultural forms are dismantled and thrust inside students' heads. So acculturation turns out to be transmission of values, skills, and information—the familiar litany from the canonical model of curriculum. The classical republican tradition of citizenry which advocates of the liberal culture movement tried to reinvigorate has disappeared entirely.

Sometimes general education advocates reject the liberal culture heritage completely. For example, Cohen and Brawer also point to its "direct application in a work setting . . . the value of their general studies as an aid to obtaining employment and to their being promoted within their career lines . . ." (Cohen and Brawer, 1987:11). Paradoxically, the defense of general education has come full circle. Although it originated at the university in opposition to the exclusive utilitarian emphasis on career preparation, that past has been forgotten. Now we find general education at the community college endorsed as achieving what it once was designed to counter.

Reformulating the General Education Problem

According to the usual rhetoric of general education reform, always looming in the future is a technical society whose members are so narrowly specialized that republican ideals of public life cannot be sustained. Forebodings of cultural disintegration gave birth to the hope for civic renewal through education—of a people both experts and citizens. Recommendations for how to achieve that range from Hirsch's insistence on teaching common cultural references, to Boyer and Levine's call to invent a humane scientific understanding of ourselves to which we all might commit, or at least that would permit our differences to be sympathetically negotiated.

Community colleges are so different from universities that approaches to general education can be appropriated only with the greatest care. But what university reformers have always feared as a possible grim future is the fundamental reality of community colleges—disarticulation between students and the academic and professional communities of our society, accompanied by mutual incomprehension and alienation.

The historic surge in enrollment that undergirded the growth of the community college in the 1960s and 1970s destroyed the traditional match between the cultural worlds of the faculty and students, and gave rise to the well-worn notion of the nontraditional student. Early theorists noticed primarily the demographic and social features of nontraditional education, rather than its cultural features, and consequently saw the whole issue mostly as remedying individual deficiencies. General education programs at community colleges can be so fascinated by those perceived student deficiencies that they end up as remedial versions of university programs.

Unfortunately, community colleges have not usually kept from going down that road. Their general education programs are typically simple distribution requirements, scaled-down versions of what is offered at elite four-year colleges—as though students' educational problem was one of scaled-down intelligence. That is inevitably how cultural disarticulation looks from within conventional educational theory, as information and skills deficiencies, or poor motivation. But a different portrait is more sympathetic and more revealing.

Remember that most students at elite colleges have a relatively easy initiation into academic and professional life. Their family backgrounds, their social network, and their previous schooling have formed them in ways to match the expectations of traditional education and point them toward academic and professional life. They have read about and can talk about intellectual matters and have done so for years; they share the attitudes, patterns of thinking, and modes of behavior which put them on a professional track

and permit them to enter into intellectual life at a reasonably sophisticated level.[2] Students at open-access institutions have not
been similarly shaped by an academic and literary culture, and so
from the perspective of that culture they are sure to look deficient.
They have almost nothing in their experience that models intellectual life, and little reason to take themselves seriously as learners
of something worth learning—a distinctively academic trait.
School is bound to seem important only in relation to its utility,
which means that they will think of themselves almost entirely as
engaged in a process of technical certification. The controversy
and debate so cherished in academic and scholarly practice certainly is mysterious and threatening; they characteristically back
away from it into an easy relativism. They have trouble evaluating
where they are relative to their goals, what sorts of changes in
themselves would be required to achieve them, or even what it
would mean to achieve them.

For nontraditional students, higher education is a profound
challenge that asks them to transform some basic attitudes and
behaviors, styles of thinking, talking, and writing. Programs modeled on the university are not likely to help and may actually
make matters worse. Not much is gained by "exposing" them to
this or that or "distributing" them among these or those courses or
divisions. Nontraditional students may be already disposed to
think of education as lists to be memorized, or a "them," the faculty, trying to get an "us," the students to believe or say they believe something. Content orientations to general education don't
try to counter those tendencies; they reinforce them. They play
strongly against the kinds of student transformations that most
need to be promoted.

General education should be the collegial response to students' cultural situation, whatever it may be. At community colleges that means responding to cultural disarticulation. Ideally,
general education should be the most basic communication from
the faculty to the students about the nature of intellectual activity
and academic life, and at community colleges that communication
is now warped and confused, a mix of uncoordinated agendas and
practices. Since the standard university versions of general education are directed toward quite different problems of quite different
students and institutions, they necessarily distort both of the distinctive problems of open-access institutions: the nontraditionality
of students and the weak, disordered academic culture.

Open-access institutions cannot perform every desirable social function or develop nontraditional students in every possible way. But they can do a much better job with the academic and career preparation of students than they now do. They can make the processes of transformation and initiation less mysterious and threatening, more meaningful, intelligible, attainable. Students need to be immersed in the complex culture of disciplines, and engaged with the practices of academics. They need practice arguing, analyzing, and talking within various frameworks with varied vocabularies and concerns, taking some questions and issues more seriously than others, and finding ways to articulate and resolve differences in perspective, interpretation, and fact.

Community colleges are not primarily in the business of developing students who might pass muster as "generally educated" from some favored perspective. Instead, community colleges should be trying to bridge the gulf of cultural disarticulation, to make academics inviting and engaging. That does not necessarily suggest students memorizing lists of information, or appreciating particular works of art—anything at all from the traditional repertoire of general education concerns. But they will have to work within academic communities, using their specific theories and methods; they will have to learn to navigate among different disciplines, different theories, and methods. Probably little harm would flow from describing this initiatory movement as "general education" if that term can be freed from its past.

The great obstacle to the initiation of nontraditional students into academic life is not their own deficiencies but the fact that colleges tend to be unselfconscious about how their curricula and practices shape students, and how academics are represented to them. We have already sketched this in a general way in the previous chapter, using the taxonomy of educational agendas. Ironically, the most startling appearance of curricular disorder is found in the humanities, where responsibility for general education is usually assigned, and institutional responsibility for maintaining norms of literacy is always assigned.

5

THE CONFUSION OF WRITING AGENDAS

THE DECLINE OF THE HUMANITIES

The humanities at community colleges are not really different from the humanities anywhere else. Everywhere traditional disciplines have grown weaker; ever greater authority has been ceded to the natural sciences and technologies. This has forced the "humanistic" disciplines into adversarial relations with the dominant scientific culture and fundamentally affected their public standing and educational role.

Although the story of the humanities goes back to the recovery of classical learning in Renaissance, paradoxically their modern formulation represents the triumph of the research university over the tradition of the liberal arts. By elevating natural science to the model of intellectual activity, universities devalued disciplines that were not engaged in cumulative, empirical research. In 1905, William Rainey Harper of the new University of Chicago argued that the sciences are concerned with explaining the existing world, while the humanities are "those subjects which represent the culture of the past" (quoted in Sullivan, 1987:23). Of course, within the utilitarian vision of education the implied question was whether the past was really worth recovering, or whether the new scientific outlook by itself could provide a firm foundation for progress and stability. In the flush of scientific and technological enthusiasm perhaps it was inevitable how the answer would go. The classical and Renaissance ideal of the scholar/humanist who strengthens republican virtue by recovering tradition was finally displaced. The new ideal was the expert, whose contribution to the common good depended on his technical knowledge of specialized fields of inquiry.

The eighteenth and nineteenth-century conviction that humanistic education was a cornerstone of democratic life was impossible to sustain in the face of social changes that reshaped education toward scientific knowledge and technical training. As their influence diminished the humanities adopted a peculiar public posture, and a rhetoric characteristically both defensive and utopian. Contemporary advocates of the humanities will appeal to the language and categories of science to justify their enterprise. But, since the traditional humanities had appealed to very different cultural traditions, that can only mean that competing conceptions now crisscross and blur, always accompanied by a torrent of nervous self-reassurance and congratulation.

At the great research universities, the disciplines of the humanities have professionalized as much as others; the weakening of the humanities is much more apparent at community colleges where the professional disciplinary associations do not artificially prop up the enterprise. The most important public defense of the humanities in open-access institutions is the policy statement of the American Association of Community and Junior Colleges (AACJC), *The Future of Humanities Education at Community, Technical, and Junior Colleges* (1986). Any policy statement from the AACJC has multiple audiences, and that will naturally tend to dilute its theoretical coherence. Nevertheless, its attempt to define and delimit the humanities is worth a careful look. The first selection is in answer to the question "What do we mean by the Humanities?"

The humanities are ways of thinking about what is human—about our diverse histories, imaginations, values, words, and dreams. The humanities analyze, interpret, and refine our experience, its comedies and tragedies, struggles, and achievements. They embrace art and art history, literature and film, philosophy and morality, comparative religion, jurisprudence, political theory, languages and linguistics, anthropology, and some of the inquiries of the social sciences. When we ask who we are and what our lives ought to mean, we are using the humanities.

In addition to the specific content of this roster of disciplines, the humanities represent an approach to learning which is characterized by certain beliefs about the value of what is worthy of our interest and study. The study of the humanities ranges from the reading of the great texts to the understanding of the contemporary, yet perennial, concerns of the human family. The methods of the humanities encompasses the methods of the particular disciplines as well as the methods of broader, interdisciplinary inquiry such as the critical and imaginative use of language, texts and other artifacts of human experience. Whether in content or method, however, study in the humanities always has as its fundamental objective to reveal that which is significant about human life—past, present, and to the extent possible, the future (1986:3).

In keeping with the practice of the federal legislation which established the National Endowment for the Humanities, the statement delimits the humanities by enumeration of specific disciplines. In an essentialistic turn, the AACJC assumes that all members of the class "humanities" must share some common positive characteristic; the diverse disciplines, it is claimed, are unified by common "humanistic content and . . . humanistic methods," by interest in what is "distinctively human," or "who we are and what our lives ought to mean."

Of course, staking out the distinctively human as the domain of the humanities is a bit tendentious. Scholars studying the history of the humanities often favor the more traditional view that the humanities comprise the study of classical Greek and Roman artifacts (or their modern analogues). Alternatively, if the humanities are set within their institutional context then what may appear most striking is the extent to which they are grouped together for reasons of historical happenstance and administrative convenience—not because they share any common nature, interests, or mode of inquiry.

Our own view is a variant of the latter. The disciplines collectively called the humanities are united only as the theoretical residuum left by the triumph of science. On one side stand the sciences—which produce hard facts, with secure methodologies. On the other stand the humanities, concerned with the soft stuff—beauty, wisdom, values—the remnant from scientific method. Such enterprises are bound to seem suspect and as needing justifications never demanded of chemistry or biology. The philosopher J. L. Austin used to call such paired notions "trouser" concepts: science, in this case, "wears the trousers" (1964).

The AACJC document then turns to the question "Why study the humanities at community colleges?"

The humanities do have inherent worth. The proper study of the humanities, however, is also decidedly practical. For example . . . higher order processes of intelligence . . . [and] skills of the mind and skills of language . . . by their very nature are especially connected to the humanities. The medium of the humanities is essentially language, and their use of language sets in motion reflection and judgment. The humanities assist in developing insights and capacities that are essential for a well-formed public life as well as a fulfilling private one . . . Community College faculty must teach the humanities to their students so that each student is better able to discover a sense of relationships among life, work, and circumstances; to understand self and society through different eyes, places and times; to reflect on the way personal origins and beliefs affect actions and values; to encounter questions and answers posed in the past; and to raise similar question about the present and future.

. . . Study of the humanities fosters disciplined approaches to questions that do not necessarily have correct answers. Study of the humanities promotes an enhanced ability to make value judgments—to select the wiser course of action. Study of the humanities inculcates a sense of common culture, encouraging civic purpose and citizenship practices. Study of the humanities seeks balance between the individual and society while fostering the basis of any civilized society—civility and mutuality.

. . . It follows that community colleges should teach the humanities to *all* students so that social cohesion may be fostered through shared understanding, language, and values. Community college students should study the humanities for a seemingly simple reason—to gain knowledge and ability to think concretely about important social and personal questions and to communicate these thoughts through clear and effective written expression.

This explanation proceeds at several different levels. First, we are reassured that the humanities are good in themselves, but that receives little attention. The real explanation argues for the humanities as instrumentally rather than intrinsically good. Study in the humanities purportedly produces an array of desirable outcomes ranging from increased "skills," to reflective understanding of self, to more competent civic participation. Not only do students individually benefit in those very important ways; social cohesion also is fostered by study of the humanities. If these impressive claims could be made to stick, no doubt a very significant increase in requirements would be justified. Perhaps it is best taken as a measure of the defensive posture of the humanities that outcomes of studying three or six hours of literature or philosophy or art have become so inflated.

The AACJC's rush to pragmatically justify study in the humanities results in a careless conflation of several distinctive conceptions of the humanities. A pitch to developing personal values and insights is in only very uneasy tension with the determination to foster social cohesion; certainly those are opposed rather than complementary, and neither has much to do with developing language skills. None of that is noticed, or at least is passed over in silence. Instead, in its brief statement the AACJC allows at least five different concepts of the humanities to be run together in a very unprofitable way. They are worth being careful about.

1. *The Humanities as Knowledge.* In its policy statement the AACJC claims that the humanities have a distinctive subject matter (finding out what is "truly human") and distinctive methods ("ways of thinking") which provide them with "content" worthy of study. However, one soon discovers that about this, whether the humanities can unequivocally be spoken of in terms of knowledge at all, the AACJC treads softly. After all, the contemporary world has few cultural resources for construing strong knowledge claims other than in the sciences. The humanities may confront fundamental questions, but what is gotten is cautiously described as "understanding" rather than knowledge. The reassurance that students should study humanities for a "seemingly simple reason—to gain knowledge" puts much greater stress on "seemingly" than is immediately apparent. The "best habits of mind" and "disciplined approaches" may be encouraged—but don't expect "necessarily correct answers." Apologists for the humanities characteristically waffle on this point, being careful neither to make knowledge claims too strongly nor to disclaim them entirely.

This timidity is best understood as the expression of the historical position of the humanities. The triumph of the scientific worldview rendered certain traditional disciplines problematic; they became "residual." Those diverse disciplines and subdisciplines, with their varied methods, objects of study, histories, and theoretical structures, with all their border disputes and disagree-

ments, are similar to one another only in that they are not something—not science. That very weak unity that is shared by all
things that are not potatoes, or all disciplines that are not sciences, is often illegitimately interpreted as a strong substantive
unity: of objects of study, of method, the modes of knowing. That
no one has every clearly specified the common objects of study,
singular humanistic methods or modes of knowing, is apparently
not really worth bothering about.

Whether or not particular humanities disciplines have
epistemic merit is a question entirely independent of the AACJC's
claims for the humanities as such. Historians or art historians, for
example, have perfectly legitimate and supportable claims to
knowledge, but not because they apply generic humanistic methods. To the contrary, if those disciplines are construed so weakly,
as just instances of humanities generically, they will be emptied of
their distinctive theories and methods, and therefore be unable to
sustain strong public claims. Were it not for the sort of epistemic
anxiety shown in the AACJC policy statement no one would be
much inclined to describe art history and literary criticism and
analytic philosophy as being all of a piece.

This first conception of the humanities has no substantive
implications for curriculum or classroom practice since by itself
it is just an expression of the fact that in the modern world humanities is a residual category. Strong educational recommendations will depend on more pointed notions of the supposed unity of
the humanities.

2. The Humanities as Cultural Recovery. Knowledge
claims of the humanities often drop from substantive knowing
about the nature of the world or of people to weaker claims about
what has been said or thought about the nature of the world or of
people. Of course, knowing about Aristotle is a very different affair
than using Aristotle as a guide to knowing about the world, but if
the latter is unavailable because of modern epistemic worries, the
former will still provide plenty of grist for a curriculum. On this
line, the contemporary significance of Aristotle or Thucydides has
nothing to do with their continuing substantive relevance to philosophy or history. It lies rather in their historical importance as
founders of the Western tradition. William Bennett goes strongly
in this direction. He insists that "the humanities tell us how men
and women of our own and other civilizations have grappled with
life's enduring fundamental questions" (1984). At the turn of the

century William Rainey Harper expressed similar ambivalence about the epistemic status of the humanities, urging that the humanities were merely those disciplines most characteristically engaged in the project of cultural reclamation or preservation.

Bennett and Harper see the humanities as a compendium of great works, as the chronicle of the cultural heritage of the West. The humanities are deflated on this account, but not eliminated. Knowledge shades into repertoire, inquiry into recovery, method into memory. The intellectual activity of the humanities need not be trivial on this account. "Reclaiming a heritage" may mean reconstituting it, recreating it through a process of reinterpretation and reassessment. However, undergraduate curricula typically shies away from open-ended critical scholarship. More likely cultural heritage will be presented as unproblematic and easily appropriated.

On the question of how the heritage is to be constituted, the AACJC is silent. But it has peculiar and conflicting things to say about why the heritage is valuable. First, the distinctive concerns of one strand of the Western philosophic tradition ("What is justice? What is courage?") are elevated to "fundamental questions that confront all human beings." These are misread as timeless questions that cut through all cultures, which exist outside of tradition and history, that confront all people regardless of time or place.

However, in a quite striking about-face, students are encouraged to reflect on "the way personal origins and beliefs affect actions and values." In other words, whatever answers anyone proposes to the eternal questions are to be drained of epistemic worth by being explained away in social scientific terms—rather than being appraised for theoretical merit. When students "encounter questions and answers posed in the past" it's not because they will learn truths about the world, or have their characters improved, or even their minds. Its merit resides in fostering "social cohesion . . . through shared understanding, language, and values." On such an account, the past cannot counsel; at best, the "heritage" is a loose compendium of culturally relativized opinions.

3. The Humanities as the Articulation of Values. The AACJC statement plays within the conventional skills/fact/value trichotomy. The sciences provide knowledge; the technologies provide skills; the humanities offer "an enhanced ability to make value judgments."

Humanities faculty work hard to establish hegemony over the values component of the curriculum. But it is a hegemony that others are only too willing to concede. Within orthodox categories, science alone offers a secure and compelling procedure for deciding among competing knowledge claims. Values are ultimately nonrational preferences, not suitable for disciplined inquiry or instruction, and elude any cognitive treatment stronger than "clarification."

Paradoxically, within science nothing is so devalued as values. Going as strongly as they do for values as being what is distinctive about the humanities, humanities faculties are unwitting partners in a characterization of their activities that completely drains them of cognitive significance. The humanities alone are forced constantly to justify themselves, to assert that they have worth, and to do it in a vocabulary that implies that whatever worth they have can't really be cognitive or intellectual.

Here, as elsewhere, the AACJC wants to play both sides. Its list of fundamental questions are all rooted in an alternative traditional vocabulary which hints at no such broad disjuncture between knowledge and values. Repeated allusions to Aristotelian and classical republican conceptions—"wisdom," "appreciation," "reflection," "judgment," and "practice"—contrast sharply with the modern notion that values are noncognitive.

This waffling about values is a consequence of the institutional history which we have already sketched. A century ago the humanities were at the heart of a liberal arts education, and provided an understanding of the role of education in maintaining a well-formed public life. When the modern research university superseded the traditional liberal arts college, it displaced the conception of private and public life which they embodied. The authors of the AACJC document, like many contemporary advocates of the humanities, share with general education reformers a yearning for "the world that was lost." But, given their modern epistemological commitments, they can find no way to hold together what looks so distinct to them: knowledge and value.

4. The Humanities as Cultivation of the Self. Sometimes proponents of the humanities respond to their devaluation by appropriating the critique of scientific rationality developed by Romanticism. The Enlightenment had modeled cognition on sensation, and value on "feeling." The Romantics rejected that, and emphasized in its place artistic categories like "imagination," "meaning," "understanding," and "insight." Romanticism tried to close the conceptual distance between subject and object, and so described meaningful human life as created in much the way artists create beautiful poems or canvases. The Artist is most fully human; a life which is denied artistic creation is less fully human; a life which does not even "appreciate" artistic creations is a bit grubby. Their importance thus elevated to the "meaning of life," the humanities can claim supervenient understandings and higher callings than are allowed to science. They "nurture the imagination" and "illuminate" the "practical demands of life."

When the AACJC introduces romantic notions and vocabulary, it ignores that Romanticism had been a self-conscious effort to supplant what were even then conventional Enlightened categories. We have already remarked on how the statement passes over the tension between the Renaissance and Enlightenment view of the humanities. Once again, divergent commitments and historical competitors are advanced as if somehow complementary rather than contradictory to one another.

5. *The Humanities as Interpretation.*   Finally, the AACJC appeals to the rhetorical or interpretive tradition as well, for whom the root metaphor is what the critic does with a text, rather than the romantic image of what an artist does with his medium, or the empiricist image of what a scientist does in the laboratory. Language, we are told, is "essentially" the "medium of the humanities" which "sets in motion reflection and judgment." By staking out language as the particular domain of the humanities, the interpretive tradition does not intend anything like literacy skills, whether higher or lower. Instead, the humanities are concerned with texts, or artifacts that may be read on analogy with texts. This allows the troublesome discipline of history to clarify its position among the humanities. As Hayden White persuasively shows, historical accounts are not neutral chronicles of past events but are prefigured according to traditional linguistic tropes such as romance, tragedy, and irony (White; 1973).

In general the AACJC statement pushes the earlier conceptions of the humanities so hard that this option receives short shrift. Nevertheless, it is hard to know how else to take the appeal to understand "self and society through different eyes" than as an interpretive movement among various theories and perspectives.- That activity certainly is not governed by the scientific method, but the humanities still demand "disciplined approaches" and "ways of understanding."

*   *   *

The debate about the humanities flows naturally within broader educational controversies. Obviously there are very striking parallels among these different ideas of what is essential to the humanities and the educational agendas charted in an earlier chapter. By the time the AACJC has finished its defense of the humanities, every single one of the educational agendas has been proposed as what is distinctive about the humanities. All the different and competing practices and pedagogies are claimed as their special preserve.

The confusion that runs through the AACJC statement is a consequence of assuming that there is something distinctive about the humanities as a group, that they must have an essential nature, be it method or content. However, no one, not the writers of the policy statement nor their counterparts at NEH, and certainly not the humanities divisions at community colleges, has been able to find any essential nature in the diverse disciplines of the humanities. Claims to uniqueness and essentiality are common but, as we have seen, these cannot be coherently sustained. That is not in itself a bad thing; it is simply a consequence of the current cultural position of many traditional disciplines. But, paradoxically, a result of the misguided attempt to find some common core of humanistic studies is the actual weakening of particular humanities disciplines within the curriculum, in favor of softer, generic, and interdisciplinary courses and programs.

The Humanities and the Norms of Literacy

The general education movement has been too weak at community colleges to lend much comfort to advocates of the humanities. The strongest push for increased requirements comes from quite another direction, from their portrayal as models of strong academic practices. If the academic culture has deteriorated by the widespread adoption of bitting practices, then, the argument goes, students will be best served by insuring that they do work in the area of the curriculum which has most resisted bitting, that has most sustained the rigor of academic practice—the humanities. However, some care should be taken here. Humanities courses may promise traditional subject matter, the reading of classic texts, and increased student writing; whether that automatically translates into strong academic practice is another matter. The actual situation is much more complicated.

Because the humanities have had such a rich history, they have developed an extremely intricate identity that now depends on a number of competing traditions. Classrooms shaped by the various conceptions of the humanities—cultural recovery, articulation of values, cultivation of the self, or interpretation of texts create quite different academic cultures. Especially, each signals different contexts of literacy, use texts differently, and provide competing models of interpretation, argument, and analysis. The complexity of texts may be simplified in various ways; they may be turned into examples of standard readings, as with cultural recovery. The cognitive status of the classroom may itself be reduced, by being turned toward the cultivation of values or personal expression. And so on.

Since the humanities have only a marginal status in the community college curriculum, none of that has seemed important. And if it were just a question of students' occasional humanities elective it actually would not be very important, or at least no more so than similar diversity and eclecticism elsewhere in the curriculum. Humanities classrooms have not taken a patent on the masking of disciplinary practices behind a cloak of the putatively generic, or the simultaneous appearance of competing and cross-cutting agendas. The trouble in humanities is just a special case of the trouble elsewhere. Its special significance derives from the critical institutional fact that the humanities are ceded primary direct responsibility for student reading and writing abilities.

What is unique about the humanities is that they now survive and thrive almost entirely because they are trumpeted as the solution to the academic problems of open access—a role they are completely unprepared to fill. Humanities divisions have managed to maintain their institutional position despite declining, practically vanishing enrollments in traditional disciplines like history or philosophy. Primarily this is because the ubiquitous problem of the academic culture is almost always interpreted as student deficiencies, especially their deficiencies with language skills. This puts tremendous responsibility on the departments charged with teaching those skills. As the problem has not gone away, English departments have expanded and composition programs proliferated. But the ambiguous heritage of the humanities is never pushed very far into the background. The competing conceptions of the humanities reappear full force in composition classrooms.

Consequently, it is a mistake to think that English departments or composition programs float above the fray, possessing subtly nuanced recommendations for strengthening the norms of literacy. Composition teachers are as despairing as their disciplinary colleagues, as lost as everybody else in the face of the continuing deep erosion of the academic culture. Like their colleagues they move about eclectically among the various educational agendas, deploying pedagogy drawn from here and there, but, it is important to emphasize, as interpreted through the multiple prisms of the humanities. The same confusion of agenda and tangle of competing practices characteristic of the community college curriculum as a whole play themselves out with full force in the department charged with the preservation and transmission of the norms of literacy.

Uniting in one teacher, or one department, or one division, the responsibility for the teaching of reading and writing, with responsibility for the teaching of humanities, inevitably blurs the distinctiveness of each. In terms of a teacher's personal history this means that she will draw heavily from her understanding of the humanities for the vocabulary in which to describe the goals and processes of the composition program; summatively, very basic disagreements and confusions about the nature of the humanities spread into the the composition program where they cannot be supposed to be harmless. The somewhat startling implication is that the division that publicly presents itself as the guardian of the norms of literacy, as arbiter and transmitter of culture, and as possessor of unique expertise in the teaching of reading and writing, is itself much more part of the problem than part of the solution.

A Guide to Composition Classrooms

A significant upgrading of the academic culture would not necessarily require that everybody agree about what counts as academic literacy; that is unlikely anyway. But writing classrooms and the general curriculum ought not be in complete disarray about it either; ought not be sending mixed signals to students, offering such confused representations of the intellectual world that students are striving to understand and to enter. Unfortunately, that really is the current situation, as the confused state of the humanities spreads systematically throughout writing classrooms.

Just as the educational agendas reappeared as different conceptions of the humanities, the focus can be narrowed further, to how the agendas play out in day-to-day writing instruction. That will be necessarily somewhat complicated; we first offer a quick characterization of each "writing agenda":

1. *Clear writing.* Writing instruction provides students with practice in the principles of clear thinking and writing which will be needed and used in their own academic work and in their daily lives.

2. *Correct writing.* Writing instruction provides students, perhaps sequentially, with the skills needed for higher-level work.

3. *Writing process.* Writing instruction maps onto developmental cognitive psychology. Thus, students are brought from the simple to the complex, from the personal to the transpersonal, from the concrete to the abstract.

4. *Expressive writing.* Writing instruction provides students with the opportunity for intellectual, aesthetic, and moral growth. Students finding their own voices is analogous to their becoming fully formed, self-aware human beings.

5. *Interpretive community.* To write is to have a voice in an interpretive community and so instruction proceeds through the creation of such communities.

Clear Writing.   Clear writing is very familiar: there are principles of thought and principles of writing, and the point of instruction is to teach those principles. When students learn the principles of thought, they can apply them everywhere, think more clearly about any subject, and communicate ideas in thoughtful, organized essays. Clear writing suggests composition courses appearing early in the curriculum, since they train students in the principles of thought and expression that cut across all disciplines.

Introduced in the nineteenth century, clear writing shaped the first formal composition programs in American colleges (Berlin, 1982). Previous generations almost always described composition requirements in those terms and taught writing according to its strictures. And that is part of its secret: that faculty and administrators, having been taught in those ways themselves, quite naturally interpret writing instruction in accord with their own experience. Familiarity now hides how complicated and problematic it really is. Traditional philosophical commitments support it; the rejection of its assumptions in this century should have undermined its authority completely—but, of course, this has not always trickled down to the classroom level.

The guiding notion of clear writing, that there are "principles of thought," has been a central feature of the Western philosophical tradition. Philosophers from Socrates to Wittgenstein, from Platonists to Positivists, were haunted by the possibility of relativism, by the fear that ultimately there might be no rational way to decide important questions. As the only alternative to that specter they proposed that the mind is organized according to the same logical principles which organize the world. It seemed that unless neutral, atemporal, and universal categories were available there could be no assurance that the world could be rationally apprehended. Education would cultivate a person's innate rationality, would bring him into closer harmony with nature.

In this century people have noticed that the philosophical tradition on which clear writing draws relies on a distinctive referential model of how language and thought relate. On that line, all language is put in analogy with proper naming. Individual words pick out, or label, objects of various sorts; sentences "picture" possible arrangements of those objects. In the paradigmatic case of proper naming, referents are familiar concrete particulars; but derivative cases such as common nouns or prepositions are seen as naming somewhat peculiar abstract objects, such as sets or essences or relations. Since in the referential account of language the meaning of words, or phrases, or even sentences, is the object or state of affairs that it picks out or posits, language instruction tends to be concerned with "clarity" or "definition" which unambiguously relate language to the objects or pseudo-objects being named or pictured. In clear writing classrooms that precise "denotative" function of language is contrasted with the messiness inherent in the so-called "connotative" or emotive function. Purging rational discourse of connotative import is necessarily preliminary to the clear representation of reality in thought. Since the mind is thought to "reflect" the structure of reality, rational inference permits movement from what is already known to new and perhaps surprising facts, so what starts as a theory of representation or reference is proposed as a powerful tool of discovery as well (Rorty, 1979; 1982).

With traditional epistemological realism in the background, clear writing puts tremendous stress on two activities: definition and logic. The relation between writer (or speaker) and reader (or hearer) is proposed as "communication," more or less successful depending on whether definition was unambiguously achieved and logic rigorously followed. For the reader the operative questions are meaning (unambiguous reference), validity (determined by rules of logic), and truth (successful unambiguous reference conjoined with correct logic).

Clear writing classrooms emphasize activities which display or elicit the principles of thought. For instance, teachers may assign anthologies of essays that provide both models of successful writing and targets for criticism. Each essay, however complicated, could be analyzed using the universal principles of meaning, logic, and communication. Typically, readings are followed by a series of questions asking students to clarify definitions, reconstruct arguments, and identify assumptions. Under the modern influence of empiricism, the matter of the truth of various positions is somewhat delicate; assumptions may appear ultimately to be ungrounded (imagine an anthology on abortion). Therefore, the most students are likely to be asked is to clarify the issues and test the options against their own experience. William Coles calls such exercises "themewriting" (Coles, 1978). Presented with an issue or controversy, perhaps reading essays from representatives of opposing sides, students "take sides" or "take a stand" or defend a "thesis." The difficulty in maintaining claims to authority forces evaluation to be conducted along dimensions of "correctness" with respect to the rules of logic and rhetoric; questions of "truth" recede in favor of "opinion."

Correct Writing.   Clear writing and correct writing each see "correctness" as the goal of writing instruction; they differ on the question of what constitutes correctness. For clear writing the issue hits at the level of meaning and logic; it emphasizes organizational, argumentative, and rhetorical principles. Correct writing conceives "correctness" primarily at the level of mechanics— orthography, syntax, and semantics. Since these are the skills traditionally mastered early in education, correct writing pedagogy recalls grade schools and high schools: drill and repetition, dictionary exercises, sentence diagramming, and rule memorization. Because of that association, these activities are a constant target for critics who charge that they trivialize instruction. Nevertheless, their use remains widespread, a special case of strategies common to rule-learning of many kinds. Clear writing classrooms often feature similar practices: things like memorization of logical rules, identification of informal fallacies, or practice with particular inference patterns.

Concern with correctness, whether mechanical, logical, or rhetorical, is in no way illegitimate or suspect. Virtually all educators evaluate student writing for correctness of spelling, grammar, or logic. What generates the distinctive pedagogies of clear and correct writing is not a concern with correctness that no one else shares, but the rather less widespread notion that rules are somehow context-neutral, that they can be taught by themselves and then applied elsewhere. According to Lester Faigley, in the nineteenth century this was the idea that elevated composition instruction to the status of academic discipline. The extraction of composition instruction from the literature classroom isolated rules of language and thought from their social context. Now free-floating, they were imagined to be logically prior, neutral, atheoretical "skills," which could be taught and mastered, preliminary to serious intellectual pursuits (Faigley, 1986:528).

The perfect institutional expressions of the correct writing agenda are learning centers staffed with reading and writing specialists and peer tutors. Here are certified experts housed separately from disciplinary departments, purporting generic expertise in the rules of reading and writing. Competence in the particular disciplines is not required, nor training, nor even familiarity with their rhetorical structures. The practices of literacy are finally completely detached from any meaningful intellectual setting whatever. Thus literacy is publicly represented as being adherence to the rules of orthography, syntax, and semantics, with occasional bows towards logic and organization.[1]

The facultative psychology of the nineteenth century endorsed independent rule instruction, but modern cognitive psychology suggests that formal rule abstraction, simple memorization, and mechanical exercises may be among the worst ways to help students learn rules. Indeed, composition faculty recognize this and heatedly eschew such descriptions of their practices. However, the most casual examination of community college classroom materials, course objectives, and exit criteria suggests the continuing importance of isolated skills instruction.

Mina Shaughnessy revolutionalized the guiding metaphors of rule instruction in composition by recontextualizing error, by emphasizing the meaningfulness of particular patterns of error. In her *Errors and Expectations* (1977), she showed how to interpret student writing to disclose their latent linguistic rules. Instead of just seeing their errors red-penciled and "corrected," students who can see what rules they are actually following are ripe to learn new, more standard rules. Shaughnessy's theory has been very influential, especially in university-based remedial programs. However, the practices she recommends are obviously both highly abstract and labor intensive. At community colleges where skills instruction already puts tremendous demands on the instructional staff, there is far less resistance among journeyman composition teachers to the more familiar expressions of the correct writing agenda: learning centers assisting with paper constructing and editing, computer-assisted skills instruction, and self-paced learning packets.

For faculty outside of the English department, writing instruction means clear writing or correct writing. When blame is assigned to composition teachers it is almost always because students cannot spell, or punctuate, or organize essays. Persistent orthographic errors are a particular bugaboo; about syntax despair reigns. Correct writing is really what establishes the sovereignty of the English department over the writing program. Other faculty do not really believe that English teachers have any special abilities relating to the principles of thought, but are happy to assign someone the dreary role of professional punctuator and sentence diagrammer. English teachers may find that role demeaning to their status as "humanists" but they recognize that their position depends almost entirely on the college-wide demand for clear and correct writing.

Expressivism.   Clear and correct writing is the guise traditional epistemology takes in the composition program. Borrowing a term from Isaiah Berlin and Charles Taylor, we call its romantic rejection "expressivism." Expressivists deeply resent traditional epistemology and classical rhetoric. Against both the constraints of eternal principles and what they see as the tyranny of convention, they affirm a radically free, uniquely valuable self, unencumbered by any rules that might inhibit its spontaneous, playful creativity.[2]

Writing activities become introspective, intuitive, and self-expressive. Since truth is identified with personal vision, the audience narrows toward solipsism.

The romantic identification of the person of the writer with the writing she produces naturally discourages close scrutiny of texts. Any criticism at all from readers is apt to be deemed in some fundamental way illegitimate. Teachers are urged to value authenticity and sincerity more highly than correctness. Consequently, to shield the creative self, traditional critical vocabulary is usually replaced by talk of "celebration" and "sharing," student writers counseled to be "true to their experience," to speak in "an authentic voice" (Elbow, 1973; Macrorie, 1970).

Traditional essay forms will be inchoately felt too confining for the full and free growth of the student's mind and feeling. Instead, faculty favor genres that can capture each writer's personal vision: journals, personal narratives, and personal reaction papers. "Bad writing [is] an echo of someone else's . . . merely taken over for the occasion of our writing . . . and good writing . . . [is] the discovery by a responsible person of his uniqueness within his subject" (Rohman and Wiecke, 1964:108). When student writing is so intimate an expression of the self it is commonly left ungraded, even uncommented upon. The teacher's role is to support, to encourage, to marvel. Some expressivists explicitly argue that writing is unteachable, that it can be learned in an appropriately supportive environment but cannot be taught (Coles, 1978). Classroom activities rely more heavily on affective than cognitive psychology. Theories of personal development such as those of Carl Rogers and Abraham Maslow are more congenial to the Romantic inclination; they are read as endorsing nonthreatening learning environments which allow students to create and reveal themselves confidently.

We have already shown how complicated relations are between concerns with personal development and the other educational agendas at community colleges. The intrusion of expressivist practice is particularly significant in developmental programs. There, it is in alliance with a social service ethos and in conflict with strong cognitive orientations. But as community colleges were "remedialized," developmental conceptions and practices diffused across the curriculum, carried most prominently by composition teachers. Although relatively few faculty practice a pure expressivism, relatively few are completely free of it either. It can appear in unexpected and somewhat surprising places.

Writing Process. Advocates of the writing process portray their practices as implied by findings in cognitive psychology. Unlike correct writing, they are relatively uninterested in mechanical correctness. Against clear writing, they drop the claim that principles of thought map reality. They share with expressivism an emphasis on the writer over the product, but, against it profess an exclusively cognitive orientation. Purveyors of writing process methods try hard to downplay those distinctions, which really don't look that important from their perspective, since they purport to offer an educational technology neutral to philosophic assumption. This stance has been largely successful; the writing process seems to offer something to each of the other agendas. For clear and correct writing the writing process is said to provide practices embodying cognitive psychological principles—the better to internalize rules of grammar and principles of thought. Expressivists, on the other hand, appreciate the inward turn that softly mutes the cognitive and communicative in favor of the creatively expressive and emotive.

For "basic writers," the writing process depends on cognitive developmental psychology, especially on Piagetian developmental theory (Emig, 1971). For writers past that stage they recommend an eclectic practice derived from research on what "experienced writers" or "real writers" do when they write. If experienced writers brainstorm, as may be uncovered for instance by protocol analysis, then students will be taught to also, at the same point in the process. If famous writers have been trained to internalize styles by "creative imitation," then many students may benefit from it also. All this, we are told, is supported by cognitive psychology, even neurology: "The reason close imitation as well as looser modeling of written materials works so well with many students is that they are 'wired' for language. This method calls on their intuitive sense of language ... Real writers ... learn to write this way" (Simmons, 1983:112).

The goal of the writing process is to promote the student's cognitive growth, to move them from "basic" to "experienced" writers, by using various scientifically grounded strategies. However, as with the canonical model of curriculum which shares this problem, the gap between laboratory findings and everyday classroom practice is so wide that psychological theory is adapted in loose, informal, and divergent ways. The result is that although the writing process orientation has displaced all others as the dominant way of talking, that has not produced a corresponding orthodoxy of practice, or even reduced the reigning heterodoxy of instructional practice. James Berlin argues that the triumph of the writing process has led even faculty strongly identifying with other conceptions to couch explanation and defense of their practices in process terms. However, he notices that eclecticism of practice continues unabated, so that reliance on the writing process may not imply very much for classroom pedagogy (Berlin, 1982). To the extent that any practices have become canonical they are prewriting, use of discovery heuristics, journals and free-writing, peer review, and multiple revision.

Interpretive Community. The interpretive community rejects the philosophical apparatus associated with the traditional agendas: the metaphysical primacy of the self dear to expressivism, and the abstractly valid principles of thought characteristic of clear writing. Under the influence of American pragmatism, its advocates describe all principles of thought, methodologies, and genres as historically situated and conditioned. Pragmatists contend that no claim of universal validity for any principle or method has ever really been made good. Consequently, in the messy theoretical diversity that comprises intellectual life, no method or principles have special standing as uniquely rational, can trump all competitors. Pragmatists do not think of rationality as obedience to universally valid principles that the world somehow imposes on the human mind. Instead, they stress the historical and anthropological view that rationality varies across cultures, and theories most usefully thought of as cultural artifacts. Thought, theorizing, and writing are simply unintelligible without both the creativity and constraint of a discourse community.

Roughly, the interpretive community takes the function of the pure creative self under expressivisim and reassigns it to the community of discourse. But the various discourse communities don't operate with a pure artistic freedom; they are constrained by a historical dialogue. What clear writing calls the principles of thought are actually the abstract rendering of the rules of that particular dialogue, illegitimately elevated to universal and apodictic validity (Rorty, 1989).

When that broad theoretical rejection of traditional epistemology is translated into pedagogy, it suggests practices designed to initiate student writers into academic discourse communities. Anthropologically, the transition from novice to competent writer is really the student's transition from "outsider" to "insider" in a discourse community (Bartholomae, 1985). Writing difficulties that appear to be the result of a faulty composing process often stem from lack of familiarity with the conventions of academic discourse (Bizzell, 1982).

Practices associated with the interpretive community are "decentralized" writing across the curriculum projects, identification of disciplinary norms of discourse and debate, and certain forms of peer review. The role of the teacher shifts from authoritative instructor (as in clear writing), or grammarian (as in correct writing), or fellow artist and appreciative audience (as in expressivism), or cognitive psychologist (as in process writing), to senior member of the interpretive community, representative of the norms and practices of the disciplinary community.

The Confusion of Writing Agendas

Each writing agenda frames the relation of language and thought in different ways; each offers a different model of intellectual activity, and offers very specific recommendations for pedagogy. Of course, composition teachers are rarely purists. Routinely, they draw vocabulary and practice from any or all of the writing agendas; inevitably, important issues are blurred or blunted. Also, researchers report a tremendous resistance to theoretical debate among classroom teachers. In an eclectic "practioners' culture," theory seems neutral to practice and to outcomes (North, 1987). The unself-conscious blending of traditions and the eclectic use of practices is a problem throughout the curriculum. It bodes particularly poorly in the department given direct responsibility for maintenance of literacy norms.

The interpretive community agenda alone insists that responsibility for norms of discourse spreads more widely. Depending on how satisfied people are with the present situation, that may seem either as a merit or a fault. Each of the other agendas suggests certifying particular teachers or departments as neutral experts, thereby stripping practices of writing and thinking of their relations to disciplinary communities. But advocates of the interpretive community view argue that the institutional position of composition departments is illegitimate. Since both writing and thinking are context bound, what has passed for generic theory and practice has actually been just the highly specific categories, genre, and practices of a particular academic subcommunity:

English teachers (Blair, 1988). The disciplinary orientation of literature instructors determines many practices of isolated composition classes—poetry writing, autobiographical narratives, or literary critiques, for instance.

The artistic concerns of the humanities are very prominent among literature faculty; they ensure that expressivism will be much overrepresented in isolated composition classrooms. However, activities like freewriting, journal writing, and little reaction papers have few analogues in the kinds of thought and expression used in most disciplinary communities, and nothing really correlates with the concern for an authentic voice. On this the various agendas are far apart. The expressivist notion that writing is primarily introspective and intuitive portrays it as mysteriously private and entirely detached from the disciplinary community and its constraints.

Since courses and classrooms are so eclectic, the opposition between expressivism and the interpretive community is not usually noticed. Partly that is because the writing agendas crosscut; thus polemical antagonisms shift with the issues. For example, the clear writing assumption that there are abstract principles of thought independent of social context finds expressivism and interpretive community allied, arrayed against traditional epistemological realism, though for very different reasons. On this matter correct writing has little to say and writing process people, as always, want to float above the debates as purveyors of neutral technology.

This is a pivotal issue, with important curricular and institutional implications. If there are abstract principles of thinking and writing, then properly trained writing instructors, understanding the principles that undergird all knowledge, could develop a neutral technology to prepare students for academic work in any discipline. The alternative is that styles of thought and analysis are strongly contextual, that there are "disciplinary cultures" that encompass varying styles of thought and expression (Geertz, 1983). That suggests that writing instruction would devolve equally on all departments, since composition teachers and departments cannot pretend to any expertise in the different styles of understanding, analysis, expression, and interpretation favored by specific disciplines.

A serious response to the crisis of the academic culture has to be located throughout the courses and curricula that are the real carriers of the students educational training. Three or six credits

of college composition, however brilliantly taught, is simply the
wrong device for addressing the general drift toward pale norms of
discourse. Composition teachers themselves often argue this point.
Isolated composition classes cannot have much impact on students'
overall educational experience if faculty in content courses ignore
or devalue sophisticated language use. The English department
cannot by itself create and sustain meaningful contexts for literacy. This has suggested the creation of Writing Across the Curriculum programs which essentially export techniques and practices
developed in composition classrooms to colleagues in other departments. To the extent that composition programs lack internal intellectual coherence, a situation which may typically be the case,
that may just spread the confusion about the role of literacy across
the curriculum under the banner of their authority.

6

WHAT'S WRONG WITH WRITING ACROSS THE CURRICULUM

The central educational problem of open-access colleges is the disarticulation of nontraditional students from the values and practices of academic life. The transition from outsider to competent member of the academic community, we have argued, is more like initiation into a new culture than the remediation of deficiencies. However, under the spell of the canonical model of education, the academic culture of the community college has itself been allowed to weaken. In Richardson's terms, texting has practically disappeared from the classroom, as disciplines have progressively bitted. In our own language, the academic culture has dissolved into an incoherent mix of competing educational agendas. Until now, the most common response to the erosion of academics has been the creation of Writing Across the Curriculum (WAC) programs: systematic institutional efforts to incorporate and sustain writing activities in classrooms or settings not directly associated with English or composition departments. Almost everywhere, WAC is praised as the most powerful, the essential strategy for strengthening academic norms.

During the last decade WAC has moved from being just another good idea to become a nationwide educational movement. The introduction of writing into disciplinary classrooms where it has mostly disappeared offers hope of creating new contexts for literacy which can reverse the tendency toward bitting. And the associated activities of WAC programs—workshops and institutes which stimulate conversations across disciplines, writing consultants to assist individual teachers, informal activities to improve writing assignments and share classroom strategies—all seem excellent ways to strengthen and revitalize the faculty and improve the quality of instruction.

121

Despite its promise, the actual impact of WAC had been mixed. It's a familiar story. Another innovation begun at the university, taken over by community colleges; programs and practices transferred to the very different academic culture of open-access colleges. As with general education, WAC at universities tries to impose a curricular unity in the face of the divisive power of the university disciplines and departments. Whatever their merits there, at community colleges, where disciplines are quite weak, the standard first-generation WAC practices have an entirely different effect. Unintentionally, they contribute to the dissolution of disciplinary norms and the weakening of the distinctive culture of disciplines.

At universities, WAC programs come in both "centralized" and "decentralized" forms. A centralized program tries to supplement and enrich disciplinary classrooms by the adoption of genres and practices used by composition teachers in their own classrooms. Decentralized programs are much less common, and usually quite controversial. Here, curricular decisions about writing fall more widely, and daily responsibility for writing instruction is carried by many, perhaps by all academic departments. The special status of composition teachers and departments is reduced or eliminated. At community colleges, decentralized programs have made almost no inroads; by far the dominant tendency has been toward programs conceived by and directed by English departments (McLeod and Shirley, 1988).

Centralized Writing Across the Curriculum is so often recommended as the way to strengthen academics at community colleges that it is important to understand how greatly its real impact diverges from its promises. Since the practices of centralized WAC programs were developed initially in isolated composition classrooms, they represent writing and thinking as generic skills, rather than as expressions of particular disciplines or intellectual traditions. WAC practices carry into disciplinary classrooms the same unacknowledged heritage of mixed educational agendas that have devastated composition classrooms. The intellectual core of disciplines can be thereby refigured, since some kinds of writing distort and trivialize disciplinary norms.

Writing as a Learning Tool

In the early years of WAC, English departments mounted missionary expeditions, preaching the good news among colleagues in other disciplines. At first that good news was inspiring, if somewhat loosely formulated. In Mina Shaughnessy's words it was a call to "increase students' involvement with writing . . . by making writing a more integral part of the learning process in all courses" (Shaughnessy, 1977:87). Over time WAC's claims became more pointed. Composition instructors, we now hear, "teach no discipline-related content but the processes of learning and writing as applied to various fields" (Simon, 1988:2). On this view, writing is a generic skill, transportable to any disciplinary classroom, be it biology or history. To teachers in those areas the promise of WAC is its alleged prowess at helping students learn better what the disciplinary professors want them to learn. Writing, said Janet Emig, and centralized writing programs came to echo her, constitutes "a unique mode of learning" (Emig, 1977:122). First generations WAC programs consequently do not suggest that disciplinary faculty alter what they do in any fundamental way, nor even really rethink the place of language and thought in their classrooms. To the contrary, WAC actually proposes maintaining current faculty practices, and is content merely to add on student activities.

The problem is that thinking of writing as a generic learning tool implicitly detaches it from particular intellectual methods, traditions, and disciplines. The social and cultural features of thought and language are given up, to be replaced by cognitive psychology and canonical learning theory. As in isolated composition classes, where disciplinary constraints don't exist, the reading and writing activities and genres that WAC emphasizes are relatively far from what a discipline thinks of as its cognitive core. The most extreme example of this loss of disciplinary relevance is also the most widespread recommended WAC practice: "private writing." In its various species, such as free-writing, journals, and learning logs, the basic idea is that students write to themselves: their ideas, feelings, questions, reactions, comments, objections.

Consider the following account, drawn from *The Shortest Distance to Learning*, developed by the Los Angeles Community College District in cooperation with UCLA (Simmons, 1983).[1] Although a manual of practice directed to disciplinary teachers, it features private writing activities quite prominently:

> Learning logs sneak up on writing. They by-pass writer's anxiety. Since they are ungraded, semi-private encounters with course material, students can write freely without worrying about the conventions they should observe in more public writing. Writing logs slip into class routine without

adjustments or major commitments on the part of the instructor. Writing can be assigned without the burden of grading . . . Generally instructors . . . [just] record the fact that
the student has done the work, and some instructors add encouraging remarks and comments. 'Correcting' a journal is
counterproductive . . . (Simmons, 1983:9–10).

On the face of it, since private writing seems so much a legacy of the expressivist writing agenda it is bound to be unappeal-
ing to most disciplinary faculty. But, the lure here is the promise
of something for nothing: great benefits to students will flow almost entirely without increasing the work load of already over-
worked teachers. The faculty's reluctance to take on additional
burdens of paper grading is offered as being in happy coincidence
with the expressivist vision of writing as uniquely, intimately personal, and the writing process account of free-writing as preliminary and heuristic to real writing. Of course, in a peculiar twist,
the problem private writing is supposed to solve is not students'
inability to write, but rather their reluctance to write. This is
traced to writer's anxiety, here interpreted as anxiety about being
graded or corrected. Apparently, students are born writers, but everywhere criticism has put them in chains. The proposed remedy
is requiring students to write while encountering only praise and
encouragement. The disciplinary community explicitly appears
only as the locus of mysterious, and somewhat illegitimate "conventions"; its only real function is the distribution of positive and
negative reinforcements.
    Probably most disciplinary faculty would be concerned about
their work load; probably far fewer care very much about students
breaking through writer's block unless they are already convinced
of the importance of writing in their classrooms. So this is where
the positive pitch for the power of writing and language in disciplinary classrooms is needed:

THE VALUE OF LEARNING LOGS FOR STUDENTS

. . . The act of writing reinforces the concepts learned. . . . A log
creates a visible permanent record.—Handy for review . . . allows students to interact personally with course materials . . .
It engages students in these learning/thinking operations.

observing	applying general to specific
recording	integrating new ideas with old

generalizing   inferring
summarizing   critiquing, questioning

... FOR INSTRUCTORS

... Awareness of what students think, feel, and understand or fail to understand.

uses ... during class:

beginning of period—review, settle down;
mid-period—define, explain term just presented;
end of period—summarize lecture or discussion (Simmons, 1983:22).

For teachers who may be little inclined toward the use of private writing, it is said to offer a stunning array of merits. Learning logs "create a record," "handy for review," useful for the imprinting and reinforcement of concepts, for retention and retrieval of information. That is important to teachers with a cultural literacy agenda. Advocates of critical literacy are reassured by the list of generic, allegedly discipline-neutral "learning/thinking operations." Those appeals are in the usual tension with expressivist calls for students to "interact personally with course materials," and with the quasi-counseling concern that writing assignments be nonthreatening. So in support of the practices of private writing we find the confluence of familiar traditions. When the cognitive psychological privileging of the private over the public merges with social service concerns about the state of students' self-esteem, disciplinary norms simply dissolve. Replacing them are adisciplinary (presumably thought to be "predisciplinary") activities which place inordinately high emphasis on isolated generic "operations," and unconstrained individual reaction.

The rub is that disciplines show no interest whatever in private, introspective, or ruminatory discourse; what counts is public discourse, informed and constrained by disciplinary norms. Unless one were in general committed to the belief that the private is prior to the public, and that this is a feature not only of expressive writing, but of disciplinary learning and discourse as well, then one would feel little compulsion to insist so strongly on the universal pedagogical merit of private jottings, on reactions and musings and whatnot (and this is true whether or not particular disciplinary adepts frequently use such devices). The argument in favor of WAC effectively concedes this point; private writing is not endorsed for its contribution to the intellectual norms of the classroom. The grounds on which the various genres of private discourse are advanced are exclusively informational, learning technological, affective, and classroom managerial. Undoubtedly those are legitimate worries; but they are not worries about the intellectual level of the classroom, or the strength of the academic culture.

The Distortion of Disciplinary Norms

However many logs and journals students write, they will succeed or fail to the extent that they learn to work within the various disciplines. But the cognitive psychological orientation of WAC inclines it toward processes and practices in which disciplinary discourse has no real place. Worse, "generic" writing assignments actually misrepresent and subvert disciplines. Consider the following, which the California text took from a class in cultural geography:

Audience: Class Instructor

Task: Investigate the origin and diffusion of at least four of your family's cultural traditions or practices.

Process:
1. Choose AT LEAST FOUR of these cultural categories for investigation: languages, religion, folk customs, food preferences and avoidances, music, holidays, housestyles.
2. Observe particular patterns in your home regarding these categories. Interview family members about their origin and diffusion. Record both your observations and interviews.
3. Summarize the geographic origins and diffusion of these family cultural traditions and practices.

Evaluation Criteria: A summary that indicates the origins and diffusion of the investigated cultural tradition (Simmons, 1983:25).

This assignment adheres closely to WAC recommendations concerning assignment design: an audience is specified; the task is broken into steps; and evaluation criteria are explicit. It instructs students directly to deploy putatively generic cognitive and writing skills—recording, summarizing, observing, and, implicitly, inferring. But what's peculiar and disturbing is how very little any of those are at the service of cultural geography; to the contrary, rigorous method plays almost no part in the exercise. In the name of generic method, students are invited—more than that they are *instructed,* to disregard elementary social scientific distinctions and methods.

The easiest place to see this is in the easy movement that is recommended, in steps two and three, from data collection to strong substantive (even if tentative) conclusions. To achieve this the assignment tells students to treat raw data as privileged and transparent; conclusions about cultural diffusion are pictured as merely summaries of participants' reports and the researcher's observations. However, no practicing social scientist would be permitted such a transition from "what they say" to "what is true" without an account of the interpretive and methodological principles that support it. Even the most positivistic social science rejects the notion that participants' reports and descriptions, uninterpreted and unanalyzed, can provide an unbiased and undistorted window onto the culture or social system. So students are encouraged, and shown by example, to ignore one of the most fundamental distinctions in social scientific method—in the name of practicing the generic skills of isolated composition classrooms, recommended for exportation by WAC.

WAC programs sometimes recognize the gap between the generic and the disciplinary. But almost never do they investigate the detailed relations between language and thought within disciplines. The luxuriant variation of styles of thinking and writing among disciplines are usually cast as relatively unimportant "conventions." On that line, for instance, thought in science must be the same as everywhere else; it is only genres that are discipline-specific, say, laboratory reports. However, language, written language especially, has an entirely different status in physics and mathematics than in literary criticism, and thought proceeds somewhat differently. That ought also be true in college classes in those disciplines. Pasting WAC conceptions of rationality onto courses relatively far from composition classrooms can only have the effect of undermining the cognitive structures of those courses.

Almost always WAC highlights the social and rhetorical aspects of disciplines over the rational and theoretical. Thus, when the emphases on generic competencies and private writing implicitly dissolve disciplinary communities, WAC recommends reconstituting them along their social dimensions, usually by the artificial creation of a surrogate audience. Consider the following assignment:

> AUDIENCE/PURPOSE: Imagine that you are one of five scientists discussed in the lecture and you are writing a letter to a colleague on the scientific milestone you have just uncovered.

> TASK/PROCESS: Your letter should include the following:
> 1. A description of the experiment you have just run.
> 2. An explanation of the significance of your finding.
> 3. A paragraph of derision about your academic peers who wrote contrary opinions during this same period of academic endeavor. (Remember to pretend that you are a respected scientist of the historical time, and this paragraph is directed against fellow scientists who previously ridiculed you.)
> 4. A philosophical statement about what you think the future holds in terms of new research horizons in the next decades.

> You may choose from among these scientists:
> 1. Pasteur and his experiments on spontaneous generation.
> 2. Semmelweis and his position on hand-scrubbing.
> 3. Lister and his position on pre-surgical scrubbing.
> 4. Mitchnikoff and his theories of cellular immunity.
> 5. Fleming and his work on antibiosis.
> 6. Edward Jenner and his work on immunology (Simmons, 1983:29).

Teachers will often say, indeed WAC explicitly says, that this sort of assignment is a creative and entertaining way to engage students in disciplined inquiry. But if this assignment is compared to the sorts it is meant to replace, it is easy to see how the stakes have dramatically changed. The assignment might have said, but didn't: "Describe Pasteur's experiments on spontaneous generation." That would be a straightforward cultural literacy approach. Or, working within one of the standard theoretical perspectives of the history of science, the assignment might have said, but didn't: "How did the experiments of Pasteur, or Semmelweis, or Lister contribute to the formation of modern biology?" That approach, which sees the past as just pointing to the present—so-called

"Whiggish History"—also tends strongly toward "tell me what I told you." Another possibility, somewhat more sophisticated, would be to ask students to interpret one of the experimenters from within a Kuhnian, or Koyreian perspective—a critical literacy approach. Quite publicly and forcefully, WAC rejects each of those standard assignment forms. Instead, students are instructed to "pretend" that they are Fleming, or Mitchnikoff, or Pasteur writing to an unidentified colleague. In such a personal communication, the typical concerns and characteristic styles of analysis of both modern biology and history of science are of dubious relevance—stronger than that, they are clearly irrelevant. The instructions to the students explicitly require them to engage in "derision" of academic peers, and "philosophical" speculation about the impact of the discovery (the latter having been already told to the student, of course). Why this peculiar and problematic exercise is thought fruitful is explained in editorial commentary:

> Casting the student in the role of the scientist writing to a colleague about his discovery . . . achieves these results:
>
> 1. The student tries on the 'persona' of the scientist, making science less remote and the writing task easier.
> 2. The student enjoys the triumph of the scientist over his detractors and is made aware of the price involved in going against the accepted wisdom of the time.
> 3. The student learns the materials in a creative, enjoyable exercise (Simmons, 1983:30).

But what is the "material" being taught in the assignment? Is it just information, classic illustrations of standard method taken from the history of biology? Is it beliefs about the relation of scientists to their peers, say, the "price involved in going against the accepted wisdom of the time"? Or maybe an attitude about how science relates to its history? In our terms, what is the intellectual hidden curriculum, the educational agenda? The answer to that is unsettling. In the name of expressivistic and affective goals, the complex history of biology, as well its social and intellectual structures, are systematically distorted. This happens because of the displacement of biological and historical methods in favor of a literary genre. The latter sees no problem with, actually values, the designation of a literally impossible audience to be addressed by an imaginary "persona."

The notion of persona has its natural home in drama and literature, where its use is somewhat technical. There, it refers to qualities of texts; it has nothing in particular to do with whether authors pretend to be or imagine that they are their characters. Nor is understanding the dynamics of scientific change, or of current scientific practice, enhanced by students, or anybody, engaging in such ruses. The point of the student's early scientific education is to begin the process of her initiation, her engagement with the practices of the various scientific communities. However rudimentary that engagement may be at its early stages it is certainly nothing like "pretending to be a scientist," the rules governing which are decidedly opaque.

Once assignments are cast in terms of persona and audience, methodological and theoretical issues are bound to be pushed into the background, as they are in this biology assignment. Even the actual social relations among scientists take a twist. The vocabulary of "triumph," "ridicule," and "derision" is so strong that it overplays the emotional and competitive aspects of the scientific community at the expense of its cooperative and rational aspects. Perhaps thinking of the history of science as great scientists battling at great price against a confederacy of dunces is a piece of inspiring imagery. But it is a serious misportrayal of the course of scientific development. Scientists and their apprentices do not think of their work in that way—only permanent outsiders do.

The intellectual credentials of imaginative projection are so poor that the real push for role-playing practices comes from an entirely different direction. The stakes are motivational and classroom managerial:

> There are some advantages to having the students write to [a fictional audience] . . . students often don't write in sufficient detail to their instructor assuming that he or she already knows everything the student might say. Writing to their 'omniscient' instructor just does not seem like real purposeful communication . . . alternative audiences and simulated situations short-cut the writing task . . . because the purpose, audience, and tone have been provided. Alternative audiences motivate students to write: they add an element of fun and creativity . . . [capturing] the student's . . . interest and [making] the learning more personal (Simmons, 1983:31).

Since the institutional appeal of WAC depends on its promise to strengthen students' overall academic experience, the relevance of worries about assignments being "fun," or "creative," or learning "more personal," is not clear. The real issue should be elsewhere, anyway: the disciplinary dimensions of a proposed practice, and its academic cultural consequences. On this point, WAC protrays the academic essay form as distant, alien, and threatening to novice writers, as rhetorically unreal. The proposed remedy is to strengthen their rhetorical situation through respecification, thereby making the assignment "real."

The theoretical point is well taken: all writing is rhetorically located; its contours depend entirely on the relations of writer and audience. If a student conceives the teacher to be her audience, she will tend to write in "insufficient detail," on the reasonable supposition that the teacher already knows anything about the subject that the student might say. Surely, different, even if fictionalized, contexts offer richer rhetorical possibilities than the tired academic essay.

On the other hand, however, students are depicted as being already so sensible about their own rhetorical situation that fictionalizing contexts seems a strange device for accomplishing that end. Attention to rhetorical principles would suggest that students treat teachers as they would any audience: by shaping the presentation to their levels of knowledge and sophistication. Realizing the fundamental absurdity of carefully crafting information for persons already in possession of it, students may offer nothing more than a cavalier coding of information, or the merest outline of an argument or analysis, for which teachers can be expected to supply an interpretation. If teachers object that essays don't go into enough detail or aren't clear, they may be hard pressed to blunt the force of the standard student retort "you know what I meant." That may be reasonable rhetorically, but it is not what teachers want.

Writing theorists know that writing assignments, traditional ones, certainly, but no less the new WAC versions, have curious social and rhetorical dimensions. Besides guiding students' initiation into academic discourse communities, teachers overtly act as gatekeepers and evaluators. This ambiguous stance greatly complicates and distorts a student's writing situation, since all intellectual considerations seem subordinate to the short-term practical task of pleasing the teacher. Correlatively, the exchange is distorted for teachers who all too easily fall into talking about writing assignments in terms of students producing "what I want." Relatively simple pedagogical strategies can ease this problem: paper graders need not be the classroom teacher, for instance. But specifying an imaginary audience, persona, or problem does not relieve the worry; it actually aggravates it. The more classroom activities highlight students producing "what the teacher wants," the less central academic and disciplinary concerns become. Students will then very reasonably cater to the idiosyncrasies of individual teachers, to role-play for them, or seem to, if that is what they want. In the name of making assignments interesting and "fun," students are removed from their real intellectual arena and dropped into a pretend one.

Morally detaching students from responsibility for their language and thought fundamentally falsifies their position in the academic community. Initiation into academics certainly is difficult and in some ways painful; students' early efforts may not be very successful. But disciplinary communities demand seriousness and engagement more than fun and creativity. Characteristically, no value at all is placed on pretending to be someone else, presenting *his* position to an imagined audience. To the contrary, the initiatory process requires that students themselves hold positions and struggle with understandings—in concert with a similarly inclined community.

Proponents of WAC claim that adopting its writing practices will help students learn whatever faculty want them to learn—across the curriculum. However, the recommended activities and genres are not discipline-neutral at all. They have a well-known history as adaptive responses of literature teachers to the isolated composition classroom. Activities such as the use of journals, learning logs, role playing, and imaginative projection have little relevance elsewhere. The best that could be said is that they each leave hanging fire the most critical educational issues: which intellectual styles students should learn, why those rather than others, and how they can be taught. But surely that is too generous. In thought, form and substance are tightly linked, and discipline-driven. Thought doesn't somehow drift independent of form, of expression. Assigning students to write in a certain form and style is assigning them to think in a certain form and style.

Collaborative Learning

Researchers studying the role of convention in composing (Bartholomae, 1985; Reither, 1985) have joined theorists in what might be called the successor disciplines to epistemology—the new history, philosophy, and sociology of science (Geertz, 1983; Bazerman, 1981; Kuhn, 1970)—in emphasizing the density and complexity of disciplinary knowledge, as well as the cultural and historical specificity of norms of rationality (Bruffee, 1984). Even within WAC circles, centralized writing programs that depend on the notion that writing or thinking are generic skills have increasingly come under fire (Blair, 1988).

Occasional decentralized university programs are built on a different basis; they are designed to initiate students into disciplinary discourse communities. Whereas centralized programs rely on generic conceptions of writing and knowing, decentralized programs try to use writing to engage students in the forms of argument, description, and explanation—the modes of knowing of the discipline. Obviously decentralized programs depend on a theoretical critique of traditional composition instruction. But, also, they require changes in the ordinary structural arrangements among departments, since English departments are publicly divested of their preeminence over the institutional norms of literacy. Neither of these is easy to come by; the latter is especially difficult. The former standing alone, theoretical critique without structural change, gives rise to another centralized practice recommended for export to the disciplines: "collaborative learning."

The basic idea of collaborative learning is that the traditional authority structure of the classroom should be dissolved in favor of "a community of knowledgeable peers" (Bruffee, 1982; 1986). In contrast to heavily didactic processes which see somewhat passive students confronting authoritative professors, collaborative learning softens the authority of the teacher through processes meant to form classrooms into discourse communities.

The most prominent advocate of collaborative learning, Kenneth Bruffee, has said that until very recently collaborative learning was practice in search of a theory (1986). He describes it in these terms:

> Learning involves shifting social allegiances. And, not incidentally, learning is therefore often best accomplished . . . not individually, but collaboratively in transitional groups or communities. The emotional stress involved in leaving one community and joining another is best borne with the help of what the women's movement of the late 1960s taught us to call a 'support group' (Bruffee, 1982: 105–106).

According to Bruffee, the practice of collaborative learning owes less to cool assessment of the relation between contemporary postfoundationalism and conscious pedagogy than it does to the socialtensions of open-access colleges. And even more so than at universities, isolated composition classrooms at community colleges have extremely weak claims to authority. In the 1960s and 1970s they underwent an explosive proliferation of survival strategies—either by attempting to bolster faculty claims to authority or by trying to get along without it. The most familiar, perhaps notorious, of these accommodations elevated students' experience and consciousness to the status of course content—expressivistic "relevance." More recently, that has been tempered by calls for a return to standards fueled by the continuing power of the clear and correct writing agendas. In contrast, Bruffee portrays collaborative learning as driven more by a social and affective agenda than a cognitive one.

The most common practice of collaborative learning is the "peer writing group." Here students are conceived to be learning from and teaching one another, by reading and commenting on one another's work in progress.

PEER GROUP GUIDE

1. Author reads paper aloud.
2. One or more members of the group summarize the gist of the paper.
3. The author tells group members particular areas of the text he would like members to focus on. The author may pose specific questions to the rest of the group.
4. Group members tell the author what they like in the piece.
5. Group members let author know what questions they have, what areas might be developed further, and what paragraphs or sentences are unclear.
6. Author tells group what his goals will be for the revised draft (Simmons, 1983:69–70).

Probably, a small group of peers following these guidelines would successfully form into a supportive affective community. The rules are designed to reduce levels of threat and anxiety, to build trust and cooperation. However, those ends are accomplished by undermining the cognitive authority of the group, and preventing it from structuring itself hierarchically, as a cognitive or discourse community would. The activities place such high value on the allegedly fragile egos of the authors, so much time is spent reassuring them, that the text under discussion can never stand on its own and be taken seriously intellectually. Because the student text is not sufficiently distanced from the student writer, the group's primary engagement is with the author rather than the text. Consequently, authorial intent decisively trumps interpretation; reader response can only take the form of blame or praise, perhaps recommendations for better embodying authorial intent. Students are told to circle around the text, to ask the author directly what he meant; that signals that what is in play is a transparent communication model: clear writing.

Rather than forming as a responsible discourse community, the student group is only acting as a stand-in for the teacher—helpful but lacking in any real cognitive authority. Notice how impoverished is the critical vocabulary students are allowed. Readers say "what they like"; they have only questions and requests for clarity, not criticisms. The text is not problematic; it carries a "gist" which students can summarize—reminiscent of the way students are taught to highlight and underline "main points" in textbooks.

In a "commenting guide," students are told directly how to read one another's writing, how to respond to a text, and by implication how to understand their own position as members of the collaborative "community of knowledgeable peers":

Remember that your main job is to offer a personal response to the pieces of writing you have before you . . .

1. Is the investigative problem clear?
2. Has the writer engaged in primary research as we defined it in class?
3. Is there a good balance of direct quotes and paraphrase?
4. Is the order of presenting findings logical?
5. Does the writer provide transitions between paragraphs?
6. If the writer lets the reader know something of his own background/beliefs, does he overdo it? Would you like to know more of the author's own point of view (Simmons, 1983:71)?

Since collaborative learning makes its theoretical appeal to the interpretive community writing agenda, its natural home is in decentralized writing programs. Here we see its practices becoming centralized by refraction through the prism of clear and correct writing. The discourse community is set to work using only the vocabulary and categories of generic thinking and writing skills. The commenting guide urges students to adopt an evaluative editorial stance toward the text, not a reader's stance. The heuristic questions do not permit the paper to be read and understood on its own terms; all invite measurement against some external standard. Occasionally, this is explicit, as when the students are asked if the paper follows the method "defined in class." But also they are instructed to deploy presumptively the evaluative vocabulary dear to clear writing: transitions, logic, clarity. Apparently, answers to the questions are gotten by simple surface inspection rather than by detailed interpretation. Uniformly, what ought to be interpretive issues appear in binary terms, in the yes/no mode, so that ambiguity and complexity are drained from the text.

One way to describe what's really happening here is that much of the dreary mechanical editorial work normally done by composition teachers in clear and correct writing classrooms has been shifted to students. In this instance, students are imagined to be saying to one another what traditional composition teachers have always said to them in the margins of completed papers: "not clear"; "logic"; "does not satisfy the assignment"; "transition needed"; "tell me more." For the purposes of justifying grades such comments have the merit of being time-honored. However, writing is necessary in disciplinary classrooms only because complex understanding and detailed interpretation reveal the intellectual structure of disciplines. Whenever classroom practices try to go around the interpretive activity of unraveling the complexities of thought embodied in a text—deciding what a paper is—to the editorial and evaluative activities of seeing what's wrong with it, how it can be made better—deciding what it is not—students are pushed a step backward. Sophisticated language use then appears more mysterious rather than less, and academic achievement less likely rather than more.

Look at the difference between these heuristic questions:

1. Does the writer provide transitions between paragraphs?
2. What relations structure the text?

The first of these asks students to decide, by quick inspection, "yes or no," whether the writer has adhered to a putative structural requirement of papers. The fix up is simple also: go back and put in transition words. The problem is that concern with "transitions" is wholly a product of the isolated composition classroom. Transitions are ways to get the reader from one thing to the next; they are primarily conjunctive relations. In nondisciplinary, contentless assignments that is doubtless a very important matter. Thought and discourse in academic disciplines are structured much more densely, however, and the relations that unify thought are necessarily much stronger than conjunctions. The second question invites a deeper reflection on the text, because it is thought and theories that are structured by relations, not just student compositions.

The various disciplines are richer, more intricate, more historically conditioned and theory bound than is recognized by WAC. Their social features also diverge strongly from those imagined by WAC. Collaborative learning, for example, focuses on the affective aspects of communities—what Bruffee calls its "support group" aspect. It ignores or miscasts the social features of the intellectual organization of disciplines. Students cannot by themselves form disciplinary discourse communities, "communities of knowledgeable peers"; but they can join them, or be initiated into them. Disciplinary communities are not free-for-alls; they are not collaborative. Socially, disciplines have strong hierarchical authority structures. Intellectually, they are driven by distinctive theories and methods. Centralized writing programs, whether isolated in composition classrooms or spread across the curriculum, inevitably misrepresent both disciplinary thought and disciplinary authority.

The Writing Across the Curriculum movement has recognized that reinvigorating the intellectual life of colleges requires, as a minimum, restoring practices of rigorous texting throughout the courses that constitute students' collegiate experience. Unfortunately, centralized WAC programs have been so preoccupied with the allegedly generic modes of writing and thinking they have championed that they have left unaddressed, even unnoticed, the distinctive educational job of open-access colleges: initiating students into the culture of academics. By now it should be evident how difficult and complicated that job really is, and how strongly it runs against the institutional grain. The natural trajectory of open access is toward progressively weaker academic practices, negotiated by students with faculty who are less and less sure of the nature and value of their academic mission.

7

THE NEW PROFESSORIATE OF COMMUNITY COLLEGES

Everybody now recognizes the new student; hardly anybody notices the new faculty. But as community colleges evolved their distinctive pedagogical strategies, curricular forms, and academic culture, they evolved also a distinctive faculty consciousness and novel faculty culture. Now, the weak and disordered academic culture of community colleges finds its perfect analogue in a weak and disordered faculty intellectual culture.

Community college faculty routinely express difficulty understanding their students—that is a simple consequence of nontraditionality. But, they have trouble understanding themselves as well. The profession of community college instructor is new, its rules unclear. Community colleges have an ambiguous position within higher education, somewhere between high schools and four-year colleges. Indeed, for a long time, high school teachers provided the largest pool from which community college instructors were recruited (Weddington, 1976). For the faculty, institutional ambiguity translates into a role ambiguity that floats unsurely somewhere between high school teacher and university professor. This plays out in everyday life in ways both large and small (London, 1980). Community college instructors have in common with high school faculty that they almost always are called "teachers," and those addressed as "Doctor" (a small minority in both settings) are thereby strongly distinguished from their colleagues. Both groups describe themselves as professional teachers or educators, and strongly disavow the university professor's strong identification with scholarship. Faculty members too publicly committed to research and publication, or displaying too much of the

139

traditional professional style, very likely will face overt charges of "elitism," and be criticized by their colleagues for not "caring" for students, for not being sufficiently "student-centered" (Sledge, 1987; Seidman, 1985).

Community college professors are drawn into and reshaped by the culture of open access, but they seldom leave behind all traces of traditional academic styles and expectations. The image of the university professor lingers for them still, though it may beckon them far less than it threatens. Peter Buttenwieser noticed this among community college faculty members he interviewed as part of a project evaluation for the Ford Foundation:

> While faculty members might not readily acknowledge it, they exhibit, almost to a person, a pronounced *inferiority complex,* which comes, I believe, from being one rung under college or university—and in quest of doctorates, publishing in top-flight journals, giving papers at prestigious conferences, and gaining recognition for academic prowess. This was the most striking phenomenon in all the conversations I had, evidencing itself repeatedly and with considerable force (Buttenwieser, 1987; emphasis in original).

Buttenwieser has interviewed only liberal arts faculty. Teachers in vocational programs don't communicate the same sense of not having made it; quite the contrary, the profession of community college professor is experienced by them as a career advance, as success rather than failure (Caldwell, 1986).

Unlike the university professoriate, both high school and community college teachers work one-step careers, evaluated, if at all, by journeyman notions of competence. Typically, faculty have lengthy, even lifelong ties to one college. With neither upward nor parallel movement available to them, professional life looms as the teaching and reteaching of the same courses, maybe even in the same classrooms. Like high schools, community colleges have extremely flat occupational hierarchies, with only few and ill-defined distinctions among staff. Journeyman instructors have no official hierarchy of competence or excellence, and no public system of recognition or reward beyond initial admission to and permanent membership in the guild. In such a system, all teachers are thought to teach equally well, or mostly so. To suggest otherwise is a serious violation of the professional courtesy expected within an egalitarian organizational culture.

But, again, community colleges are ambiguous institutions. They characteristically retain at least some traditional collegiate forms; hardly any obliterate all traces of academic hierarchy. However, practices such as tenure and promotion, a system of academic rank, and formal recognition of distinction, where these exist at all, are unlikely to be linked explicitly to scholarly accomplishments, or even success in the classroom, since the former are thought irrelevant, and the latter impossible to evaluate. Public distinction is more likely bestowed for "service to the college," for longevity, or simply to guarantee roughly equal distribution of recognition among departments and divisions. To community college faculty, the whole concept of academic hierarchy that permeates the university seems to smack of the twin evils of arbitrariness and elitism.

The interesting and paradoxical corollary is that faculty at "teaching institutions" resist evaluation of teaching as inherently suspicious, as necessarily subjective and capricious, the first step on the slippery slope away from "academic freedom." Perhaps that resistance comes from a natural desire for autonomy or is just a fear of being found out; but it has deeper cultural sources in the code of the guild. The journeyman illusion is that all faculty members are created equal, be they part or full-time, Ph.D. or B.A., published or not—one might even say competent or not, since the defining feature of a journeyman system is that competence is entirely a matter of initial certification. A faculty so organized naturally splinters: toward isolated and autonomous jobbers with no professional future beyond maintenance of membership in the guild, toward loss of corporate identity.

Earl Seidman's *In the Words of the Faculty* (1985) sketches how faculty experience their work situations and career prospects in the face of the transformations that open admissions wrought within community colleges. He portrays community college teachers as beset by uncertainties and torn by ambiguities in a professional role that wavers somewhere between traditional college professor and traditional high school teacher. His picture is of frustration and isolation, of progressive detachment from graduate disciplines fostered by the elevation of teaching over research, and the Sisyphean struggle to satisfy the powerful community college imperative of "student centeredness."

For Seidman, the small daily crises of community college faculty and their more global role ambiguities and tensions are symptoms of institutional and political failures of higher education.

Though community colleges took on the task of democratic education, endorsed in word but largely renounced in action by traditional institutions, the underside of open access has been that they remain at the bottom of the academic status hierarchy. Denied respect as academics, community college faculty self-define as teachers, rather than as sociologists or philosophers, and turn to a student service ethos to understand the nature of their profession. Thus, community college "professors" are pushed ever farther from the disciplines they originally professed.

Of course, role ambiguities hit teachers of the traditional liberal arts much harder than their colleagues in vocational programs. Many of the latter are drawn from vocational schools and industry; both socially and economically they experience their new positions as personal advance. Typically, they report high levels of job satisfaction, and low levels of dissonance. Partly, this is because they come with very different expectations about their role, which plays on one side of the dissonance, but, also, their experience actually is very different. While liberal arts faculty typically see students for only one semester, perhaps teaching "service courses" for vocational students or introductory courses for which there are no corresponding advanced courses, their colleagues in career programs have much more sustained mentor-like relations with students. Within the structure of their programs they are able to experience student growth and success over time (Richardson et al., 1983; Caldwell, 1986).

However, for teachers of literature, psychology, philosophy, physics—for teachers of the traditional academic disciplines—a career line consists of introductory level courses, four or five, at some places even six per semester, taught over and over for twenty, thirty, or forty years. Joined with the tensions and dissonances of the new teaching role, the faculty's disengagement from disciplines spawns a progressive, if silent, academic drift—away from rigor, toward negotiated anemic practices. For any individual teacher, disciplinary concerns rather quickly recede under the pressure of classroom necessity, to be replaced by the approved professional concern with "teaching." If they share nothing else community college faculty members share that initiatory experience.

Thus, disarticulation and nontraditionality cut two ways. The new student now encounters a new professoriate. On that everybody is agreed. However, its newness is perhaps less a matter of being "student centered," or "exclusively committed to teaching," as in the reigning ideology, than a matter of the confused reshaping of traditional professional models, and the loss of corporate norms, identity, and mission. Still, the striking mismatch between traditionally-trained faculty and a nontraditional career has been long recognized almost everywhere. In response, community colleges have made routine staff development activities ever more ordinary, and more prominent, features of their institutional landscape.

"Developing" Individual Teachers

The problem of the academic culture is not a matter of the personal qualities of either students or faculty, whether individually or in sum. Similarly, what is distinctive, and disturbing, about the new professoriate is not so much their personal professional qualifications, predilections, abilities, and styles, than the social and cultural features of the new profession. However, just as we have seen the educational issues of community colleges always recast in terms of individual students, so ordinary staff development activities also are conceived as trying to influence teachers only individually, or, at best, in aggregate. Individual faculty members are the target: the intention to make them more informed or better teachers, even happier people. By now, that should be familiar as the way deep cultural issues can reappear, twisted and thrust into the heads of individual persons, in this case teachers. That kind of lens is bound to distort the cultural picture. Still, standard practices notice things worth noticing.

1. *Workshops to Counter "Burnout."* The last twenty years have seen an amazing proliferation of in-service activities with a strong therapeutic and social service orientation, designed to help faculty better understand and manage the normal transitions and stresses of career and personal life. The days of "T groups" and experiential workshops are now mostly behind us, but many workshops still are touted as offering sensitivity training, stress management, personal development, and so on. Additionally, in keeping with widespread corporate practice, colleges are now more frequently implementing Employee Assistance Programs featuring drug and alcohol intervention, counseling, and "wellness" workshops.

Such programs may focus directly on "burnout" (a feature of the one step career), or "middle-age crisis" (a concern primarily because of the so-called "graying of the faculty") or maybe just the

teacher stress that flows from the unusually intense professional/
client exchange demanded by "student centeredness" (Seidman,
1985). All implicitly recognize that deep tensions and ambiguities
in the faculty role produce high levels of stress, dissatisfaction,
and disengagement. But rather than encouraging reflection on the
nature of the role, a social and cultural matter, workshops inevitably redefine the issues as internal to the individual faculty member. The college faculty again is imagined to be an aggregate of
independent journeyman, each individually to be addressed by
therapeutic activities to improve his well-being.

Were faculty understood not so much from under the skin,
but culturally, their real situation would be better displayed—the
overall shape of their professional lives, how they understand their
professional role, and the way they are influenced by the organizational culture they both share and shape. That would move the
level of analysis from the aggregate psychological to the structural
sociological and interpretive anthropological. If staff development
"facilitators" were drawn from the ranks of organizational theorists rather than psychologists, there would be many more attempts to influence the faculty culture by affecting the intellectual
and social environment, the structures within which faculty act.

2. *Sending the Faculty Back to School.*   The traditional
graduate training of community college faculty typically is much
more limited than their university counterparts, and their continuing disciplinary identification is certainly very much weaker.
Many fewer than twenty percent of community college faculty hold
the doctoral degree, even in traditional liberal arts disciplines; few
engage in scholarly research and publication. Although those demographic and social features of community college faculty are
sometimes the consequences of consciously chosen administrative
policies (Sledge, 1987), nevertheless, many community colleges offer incentives to their faculty to continue or return to graduate
education. They may provide tuition remission or reimbursement
for graduate course work, released time or study leaves, perhaps
even sabbaticals.

Since community college instructors have neither need nor
opportunity to teach the fine details of their graduate specialities,
the relevance of strong scholarly abilities and interests for their
day-to-day work has always seemed dubious (London, 1980;
Sledge, 1987). The tendency has been to think that disciplinary
expertise roughly equivalent to a graduate teaching assistant's is
sufficient for staffing the introductory level course—the staple of

the community college general curriculum. Encouraging faculty "back to school" therefore seems a bit puzzling until it is recognized as expressing a minority report on the still unresolved issue of the relation of academics to the open-access classroom. Perhaps, some would say, we don't need journeyman experts who can be counted on to routinely teach the basics from a multicolored textbook. Perhaps the exact reverse is true, that extraordinary knowledge and understanding of disciplines is needed for effectively teaching in the community college.

At the university, lower-division introductory or survey courses have a clear and well-understood place in the curriculum. They entice students toward majors, or they provide a background in a discipline for students pursuing other majors, or are part of general education requirements. However, at open-access colleges, these avowed purposes have a somewhat hollow ring. Only a tiny percentage of students in any classroom will actually major in the discipline; perhaps nobody will. Most students will leave college before they have the opportunity to major in anything. That is the context for the informal renegotiation of course rigor and course content which is so familiar. Faculty members who are relatively undereducated in and professionally disconnected from their disciplines, and without ongoing research interests, are unlikely to be able to represent their discipline intelligibly to nontraditional students, to interpret its intellectual structures, theoretical models, and vocabulary, to locate its concerns relative to others, and so on.

Community college curricula need not be arranged as disciplinary matrices; the question of the relation of individual disciplines to curricula, and to student educational experience is hardly ever debated. And, staff development on the "back to school" model actually reinforces the tendency to think of disciplinary courses and disciplinary information as being at the heart of the community college curriculum.[1] However, for as long as that arrangement remains the norm, more powerful and quite different programs of disciplinary education and professional involvement seem necessary for strengthening the intellectual norms of the average classroom—though by themselves they are surely insufficient. For individual teachers, finishing degrees is certainly a worthwhile endeavor. However, the institutional impact of the relatively few is somewhat more problematic.

3. *Developing "Effective Teachers."* The proudest claim of community colleges has always been that they are student-centered teaching institutions. As community colleges were largely

shaped by this vision, so also their faculties developed professional identities divorced from scholarship and disciplines, new identities as effective teachers, the vanguard of an instructional revolution. With this came a new notion of faculty development; the new profession was to be single-mindedly concerned with the improvement of instruction. In keeping with that orientation, the most common professional development activities at community colleges purport to help individual faculty members improve their teaching.

The new profession, "effective teacher," was made possible by the assumption that pedagogy can be meaningfully separated from the various disciplines, that teachers might be experts in teaching and learning understood generically. Cognitive psychology would provide the model for effective teaching. Members of the new profession typically are urged to respond to the special needs of nontraditional students by gaining expertise in the instructional process. In particular, teachers are told to learn such things as specifying objectives and organizing courses into carefully arranged sequences for mastery by students. Similarly, "learning packages" are endorsed, as is computer-assisted instruction and other forms of individualized learning. This has been the primary focus of in-service sessions and curriculum development workshops for the past twenty years.

By now it is a familiar line, drawn from the canonical model of education, and with it dependent on the epistemological and cognitive psychological assertion that the processes of teaching and learning can be independent objects of knowledge. On that assumption, the professional development staff really have something to teach faculty, and one would expect them to adopt a stance analogous to that of the faculty to the students (i.e., expert to novice, teacher to learner). However, hard-working, strong-willed, and battle-tested faculty so strongly resist claims to superior expertise from anyone who would teach them how to teach that staff development on this model is always fraught with tension and anxiety. Having to play on that court, staff developers characteristically adopt a softer pose: "facilitating" faculty growth, "sharing" expertise, "celebrating" diversity. But although that now seems to everyone the natural way to proceed, it is actually quite peculiar that at colleges that self-define as "teaching institutions," public claims to theoretical knowledge of teaching and learning can appear only so tentatively, so weakly, and so much in constant worry of being trumped by the everyday experience of individual classroom teachers: "practitioners."

The Spread of Practitioners' Culture

The familiar models of staff development all conceive community college faculties as aggregates of individual teachers, each independently struggling with the concerns and frustrations of his
role. Staff development activities attempt to affect colleges by influencing individual classrooms, and that by changing individual
teachers. The magnitude and audacity of that effort has always
been daunting, and the likelihood of success a bit spare, but it has
seemed the only route for really changing students' classroom experience. Unfortunately, just as the canonical account of education
entirely ignores the social and cultural features of student transformation, the familiar staff development processes utterly disregard the sociocultural condition of the faculty. In fact, faculties are
more than aggregates of individual teachers. The initiatory processes of disengagement from disciplines, and reengagement
through classroom practice, create a peculiar, but still recogniz-
able form of professional culture.

"I am an independent contractor in my classroom," said one
of our colleagues recently; "we are all independent contractors."
His picture of a community college faculty was of an association of
independent journeymen, each sovereign in his classroom, joined
only by such informal agreements as such weak social arrangements are able to support. However, although community college
faculty imagine themselves in the natural condition of a professoriate (our colleague's remark was enthusiastically endorsed by
everybody present), their situation is actually quite novel, a consequence of the particular evolutionary path traversed by open-
access institutions. The forces that have shaped the distinctive
community college professoriate are often remarked upon, if the
details inevitably vary from here to there: a typically large reliance on part-time teachers, faculty unionization, the drive for educational technology and "learning packages," the weakening,
even the disappearance of courses beyond the introductory level,
the geographical fragmentation of colleges into numerous community sites, and so on. Almost everything about their situation
pushes community college teachers apart from their colleagues,
and shatters their corporate identity.

Sharing a commitment to teaching, but without a shared notion of what effective teaching might be, with strong affective ties
to one another, but without the intellectual guidance and constraint provided by disciplinary cultures, faculties take on the as-

pect of a "practitioners' culture." They come to undervalue intellectual exchange and mutual criticism, and to overvalue "sharing" as sources of professional and organizational development (North, 1987). For the institutions themselves, facing the most difficult job in higher education, the consequences are debilitating. Operating within the rules of practitioners' culture, colleges cannot bring their collegiate intellectual resources to bear on curricular or educational problems. In fact, since intellectual issues come to look like political issues that call only for political adjustments among contending parties within the society of journeyman equals, colleges effectively deny that they actually have corporate intellectual resources. They will be unable to conceive their problems at any level higher than the individual classroom. Thus, when colleges imagine themselves to be aggregates of individual teachers, their wishes will come true.

For people who have not lived within a practitioners' culture, it is hard to imagine; and no ethnographic research as yet adequately details the community college faculty culture. So we now offer two descriptions of faculty interaction, two stories really. Insiders will recognize the pattern, and outsiders begin to get a sense of the malaise afflicting the community college professoriate. The first story takes place within the walls of a single community college (Seymour, 1989); the second at a national conference among instructors who had never before met (McGrath and Spear, 1987).

In the first tale, an instructor had invited his colleagues to join in a series of workshops to engage one another in theoretical debate on "the reasoning behind our method" in remedial reading courses. The announced plan was for an initial presenter to focus on "the underlying philosophical assumptions which drive our teaching of Reading courses," and then have two respondents comment on that presentation.

However, the very first workshop departed from that plan in classic practitioner style. The presenter, Mary, began with a story that produced smiles and nods of approval among the dozen or so participants. Several years earlier, as a graduate teaching assistant assigned to teach her first reading course, Mary had expressed concern about her lack of training. She had been immediately assured by her faculty advisor "that teachers with graduate degrees in Reading don't know any more about how to teach reading" than Mary did. She reported being told that a personal enjoyment of reading and a desire to get students to experience that enjoyment themselves were the real keys to good teaching of a reading course.

Mary then described her initiation into the ranks of community college reading teachers. From the start, she said, she had rejected standard reading textbooks that had students read paragraphs and answer questions about them. Instead, she adopted an impressive array of activities—geared to achieve basic reading skills, of course, but also aimed at developmental objectives. She listed them: students gaining familiarity with the library and learning basic research techniques, achieving self-awareness as well as cultural literacy, learning cooperation with other students and respect for ethnic diversity, gaining self-esteem, and more.

The first respondent, John, asked the moderator if he were really required to respond to Mary. The moderator replied that he was not. John then proceeded to describe in detail how he conducted his own reading courses. In other words, for John, discussing teaching meant "sharing"—a term never used lightly in practitioners' culture. The college, in his view, was just physical space, the faculty a collection of private practitioners. "I am an independent contractor . . . allowed to use the classrooms [here] for my teaching," he claimed. The activities and objectives John listed were somewhat different than Mary's but within the sharing relationship; there was no way to pointedly formulate their relation— whether they were opposed or complementary, for instance. In fact, that issue did not seem important to John.

The second respondent took a somewhat different tack. Henry tried placing his own teaching in relation to that of the other speakers. John, he said, was at one end of a spectrum, trying to cultivate the students' inner voices. In contrast, Mary was in the middle and he, Henry, was on the opposite side from John, attempting to expose students to an "outside," to Western culture itself—in the form of Homer's *Odyssey*. Although he did not work it out in any detail, Henry's "spectrum" might have shaded from subjective to objective, or Romantic to Classic, or perhaps expressivist to social functionalist. The implication of his remarks seemed to be that very deep, if muted, theoretical conflicts existed among the three presenters which might have important educational implications. In any case, Mary's emphasis on academic routine, Henry's on reading the classics of Western literature, and John's on personal liberation do seem seriously at odds.

But Henry's attempt to construct a grid to map differences in practice onto differences in theory met with an extremely strong negative response from the audience. The first to speak set the tone. For all the apparent differences among Mary, John, and Henry, the similarities, he said, were really much stronger. All three established "comfort zones" for students, and all developed "customized approaches" appropriate for community college students. Immediately, other participants, including the presenters, rushed enthusiastically to assure everyone that the three accounts actually revealed far more similarities, what they called "commonalities," than differences. They listed some: all used reading aloud; all had their students copy material from books; and all emphasized questioning. That, as it turned out, was the end of the discussion devoted to theoretical issues about the teaching of reading. The rest of the time was spent telling classroom stories, success stories mostly, but occasionally cautionary tales about how impersonal institutional and social forces undermine students' efforts.

Perhaps it is natural that co-workers whose professional lives are spent in close proximity will develop social processes for defusing potentially explosive debates. So, our second story throws the net wider; it tells of community college teachers at a national conference. Each had been invited as an articulate spokesperson for a familiar approach to teaching reading and writing. They had never before met, nor, as far as we know, ever met again. The format of the conference was for several preliminary sessions in which each speaker would make a formal presentation, followed by a plenary session which would bring everyone together for debate.

Mostly, the speakers broke out along the lines uncovered in our previous chapters. One appealed for readings drawn from the cultural canon. Strangely, the reason given for this was from classical aesthetics, that apprehension of beauty is definitive of our humanity and therefore should not be denied to community college students. The second speaker insisted that texts and writing assignments should be chosen with a view to heightening students' personal, social, and, especially, political awareness. The reading and writing classrooms' claim to be "liberating" was offered quite literally. Students were portrayed as struggling, under the guidance of a politically aware faculty, to appreciate their own position as black, Hispanic, female, or working-class. Now although the speakers on this first panel were as opposed as right wing and left wing educational views can be, in the cross talk portion of the session they were content to deny their differences, actually claiming that they agreed about all important matters and were just pursuing alternative routes to the same goals.

The second set of speakers each went a different way. One argued that skills development, the traditional goal of remedial education, is best conceived as an exercise in linguistic anthropology. Students and teachers can be partners in research, the goal of which is the students' achieving competence in a new language community. This speaker joined in the polemic against "mechanical" methods, the explicit bogey of the earlier session, and stressed that literacy must be understood as embedded in a tacit tradition of textuality. Perhaps the existence of a common polemical opponent and the analysis of literacy as partly constituted by traditions of canonical texts masked the differences between this speaker and the others. But an account so self-consciously proceeding within a social-scientific framework ought to be at pains to distinguish itself from accounts coming from traditional aesthetics or from romantically conceived notions of personal liberation through political action. But alas, that was not to be.

The final presenter tried to understand the problem of remedial education using primarily literary categories. What, he asked, are the "stories we tell our students, and ourselves?" What narrative can find the personal, social, and moral meaning in an enterprise that the surrounding culture defines as failure? None of the approaches of the previous speakers seemed to him to touch this fundamental issue.

The plenary session was begun with remarks by a respondent who commented globally on the various speakers' relations to one another. The scene that followed is reminiscent of our earlier story, though on a larger scale. Very quickly, all rejected the characterization that they were in any real theoretical opposition at all, certainly not fundamental opposition. They began to tell stories about their colleges and their students, to find areas of commonality. The audience joined in. After a while the moderator thanked everyone present for sharing their experiences, and the session was adjourned.

These were all good and caring teachers, not deadwood, but among the best. All had gone far out of their way, in the second story hundreds or thousands of miles out of their way, ostensibly to argue, to debate, to make intellectual progress together on some of the most critical issues of their professional lives. Why is it that such important conversations short-circuited so quickly? The quick answer is that among community college faculties, unlike university faculties, social organization does not follow the academic/intellectual organization. The elevation of teaching over research or scholarship may have turned faculty into "generic teachers," but it also stripped away any intellectual norms that might bind them together. And so they search for commonalities, or in any event don't raise matters they see no rational way to resolve.

One by one, individual teachers are drawn from their disciplines and initiated into community college culture. Maintenance of disciplinary ties is extremely difficult; everyone notices that. Teachers are not expected to write; few do. More important is that exchanges among community college faculty are not characteristically written. They are spoken, experienced, shared. Put differently, teachers share what is primarily an *oral* culture. Paradoxically, although highly educated and literate, they are, relative to one another, "more comfortable in the person-to-person human lifeworld than in a world of pure abstraction" (A. R. Luria; quoted in Ong, 1982:53). This is why community college faculty are such storytellers. As Walter Ong notes regarding oral cultures: "Oral cultures tend to use concepts in situational, operational frames of reference that are minimally abstract in the sense that they remain close to the living human lifeworld (1982:49)." Released from the intellectual norms and social constraints of writing practices, the faculty culture "concretizes." Teachers grow deeply suspicious of "abstract theory," and turn to experience, to classroom practice, as the only things really worth talking about.[2]

So the community college practitioners' culture provides but meager resources for persuasion; it accords only very weak status to theory, analysis, and debate. Inevitably, precedence is granted to anecdote over theory, and to informal classroom experience over rigorous method as sources of knowledge. Stephen North calls this form of knowledge "practitioners' lore" and describes the social rules governing it like this:

> Anything can become part of lore. The only requirement for entry is that the idea, notion, practice, or whatever be nominated: some number of the community must claim that it worked, or seems to work, or might work . . . contributions to it have to be framed in practical terms, as knowledge about what to do; if they aren't they will be changed (North, 1987:24–25).[3]

Within a practitioners' culture the conscious link between theory and practice is broken. If and when theory is proposed, it is treated as something to be mined for practical suggestions, for what to do in class on Monday. Likewise, when a new course, a change in policy, or a new curriculum is debated, anyone who says

"I tried that in my class last week and it worked just fine—or didn't," cannot be meaningfully debated with, certainly not refuted. No public rules can decide among practitioner claims because they don't seem to compete; they seem instead to complement, or supplement one another. That is why lore just piles up in a way that disciplinary knowledge does not. Nothing can ever really be left behind; teachers just accumulate more and more techniques to choose from. Since the social demands of practitioners' culture are such that sharing is the approved mode of interacting—criticism being forbidden—nothing can stand against that ace of trump: the everyday classroom experience. Certainly theory cannot; that has to seem mere speculation, perhaps personal bias, at any rate far inferior to personal experience, and anecdotes about that experience.[4]

Toward a New Faculty Culture

Many recent calls for reforming secondary education have focused on the role of teachers in developing effective schools. The typical high school teacher has few opportunities for intellectual challenge and stimulation, support for professional growth, and little control over decision-making in the school. Advocates of "effective schools" argue that to improve public education schools should work to overcome the isolation of teachers by creating a collegial environment which provides opportunities for staff interaction, and helps teachers view their colleagues as sources of ideas and support (Lieberman, 1988). Studies suggest that schools characterized by high levels of staff interaction develop shared professional norms and have more faculty involvement in instructional planning and practice (Little, 1982; Van Maanen and Barley, 1984).

In comparison with the average high school, most community colleges appear to have a professional culture. Individual teachers exercise considerable autonomy in the classroom, and governance structures permit faculty significant influence over curricular and other academic matters. However, the comparison with high schools has tended to blind commentators to the peculiar academic culture which has developed in open-access institutions. The startling features of the professional culture of community colleges—the studied insistence on avoiding even the appearance of disagreement, the continuing search for areas of commonality, and the dread of irresolvable conflict within a society of equals—have no real analogue among either university professors or high school teachers.

The disordered academic culture of community college is the perfect expression of faculty that have become unable to sustain strong academic practices among themselves, whose professional culture is organized primarily along social rather than intellectual dimensions. A powerful academic culture can be created and sustained only by a faculty that is itself organized according to academic and intellectual rules of discourse and decision.

Since the institutional and social forces weakening the intellectual culture among faculty at community colleges are unlikely to lose their influence in the near future, community colleges should work seriously toward constructing activities which encourage and sustain academic practices among the faculty as a collegiate body. If the educational problem of open access is how to initiate nontraditional students into an academic culture, the first order of business has to be ensuring that a strong academic culture exists in the first place. Realistically, relatively little can be done to reengage faculty in their original disciplinary communities. But much can be done to help faculty reengage one another as intellectuals, as members of an academic community, to rediscover the excitement that once drove their own academic careers.

Schools cannot be fundamentally improved by trying to change faculty members one by one, by exhorting them to whatever teaching techniques happen to be approved by reigning educational theories. The more important point is that schools cannot even be changed that way, since that is their current condition: individual teachers struggling alone in the open-access classroom, taking teaching tips from wherever they may be found. It is not always easy to distinguish mature professional autonomy from finely honed eccentricity; but strengthening individual classrooms, the heart of students' academic experience, surely means strengthening the institutional academic culture in which they nestle. And that is something no "autonomous" teacher, however gifted and good-willed, has control over; the problem is ourselves together, the solution ourselves together.

Afterword

RENEWING THE ACADEMIC CULTURE

As professors, teachers, we have lived our professional lives inside community colleges, and been touched by their idealism. So, if we are critics of community colleges, we are sympathetic critics. More so than university researchers, more so than legislators or policymakers or college administrators, to us, to teachers and students who come together at community colleges, it makes a difference that they be understood, and reformed—that they be made to work. That is why our account is so impatient with the usual, ideologically driven, insiders' rhetoric—that community colleges are already wonderful, that they already work fine, that all they need is some fine-tuning. Change begins in self-knowledge; nothing obstructs change quite as effectively as self-satisfaction. The problems of community colleges, of all open-access institutions, go much deeper than is ordinarily recognized; solutions will have to as well.

Although our analysis of the academic crisis of the community college has pursued historical, theoretical, and meta-theoretical issues about curriculum and pedagogy, as well as organizational and cultural issues about faculty and staff, it must always be held closely in mind that the students are what community colleges are about. Fulfilling the promise of democratic education is what they are really about, if they are really about anything. That they should have stumbled and lost their way is not surprising. From the beginning theirs was the toughest job in higher education— one that nobody else wanted to do, was prepared to do, or had any idea how to do: educating nontraditional students.

For nontraditional students, college seems a place where they don't really belong, where they don't expect to succeed, and where, in class after class, they are asked to do peculiar things for reasons they don't quite understand. Academic life is experienced by

155

them as culturally strange and unintelligible; they are "disarticulated" from the norms, practices, and styles of academic life. This is both the central feature of open-access education and its greatest challenge.

Any college is the meeting place for the faculty and the student cultures. But, in the complicated ways that we have sketched, both are implicated in the breakdown of academics in open-access institutions. Students are carriers of nonstandard cultural styles—opaque and mysterious to faculty who interpret what they see as deficiencies. On the other side, the faculty has lost its cultural unity and vitality; it stands as the sum of diverse and competing educational aims. Faculty and students communicate through the curriculum and in the classroom—a communication that is distorted and confused by the brew of educational agendas that we have uncovered. If outcomes are to be dramatically improved all that has to change.

Individual colleges obviously are constrained in many ways—although perhaps not so many as they profess. Our recommendations for strengthening the academic culture at individual colleges try to have a lively sense of the possible, and play entirely within everyday constraints. The historic forces that shattered the academic culture of the community college might be simply wished away, but it is unlikely they will simply go away. So, we don't suggest large bureaucratic restructuring, nor imposing requirements that seem onerous to nontraditional students, nor formally deemphasizing disciplines, nor trying to convince large numbers of strong-willed faculty members to change their teaching styles. We don't think such reforms are really possible on individual campuses; and in any case, they do not address the central educational problems of open-access colleges: the disarticulation of nontraditional students, the confused and disordered curriculum, and the weak faculty professional culture. To the extent that these can be addressed by community colleges alone, we suggest some ways to clarify and strengthen the professional culture of the faculty as well as the student academic culture, and to reorder curricula to render explicit and intelligible the intellectual hidden curriculum—none of which, of course, can be done very effectively without the others.

Rebuilding the Faculty Intellectual Culture

Teachers, many of whom have been at the same college for many years, often treading and retreading the same courses each semester, cannot be expected to change dramatically. Nor is it especially sensible to think that the crushing problems of the open-access college could be much alleviated by individual teachers becoming more skillful or more sensitive in the classroom. Improving the overall academic culture and the quality of teaching and learning will call for new relationships among significant numbers of faculty, partly so that teachers can support, encourage, and sustain one another; but more importantly so that faculty can join together to create a vigorous academic setting for students. We know of no magic bullet that can be fired at this problem. At best, renewing the academic culture among faculty will be a difficult and lengthy process.

1. Strengthening Ties to the Disciplines. Standard staff development practices frequently recognize the progressive disengagement of community college faculty from their graduate disciplines—a problem that is most critical in the traditional liberal arts. Present efforts to reconnect faculty with disciplines can be strengthened in several ways. First, without any fear of displacing teaching as the central professional role, colleges can undertake to encourage professional involvement in the disciplines, and, perhaps more important, to legitimate scholarly activity among the faculty. Membership in professional associations, attendance at disciplinary meetings and conferences, participation in NEH or NSF professional development seminars, ongoing research and publication—these should all be institutionally supported and rewarded rather than discouraged through benign neglect.

It has been a very serious error to think of the profession of teaching at community colleges as the job of journeyman practitioners. More even than at universities, the central professional challenge is to render the disciplines intelligible to outsiders, to initiate them into its mysteries. This implies that faculty need a high level of continuing involvement with disciplinary communities. Otherwise, the very real danger is that they become outsiders themselves.

2. Building a Faculty Intellectual Community. The real problem about the faculty is not individual qualification, or levels of commitment. It is the phenomenon of the practitioners' culture-which plays so strongly against rigorous analysis and public debate of important educational issues. To counter that, faculty have to become reaccustomed to encountering each other as intellectuals, and not just as fellow practitioners. At present, community colleges lack institutional settings in which that might occur.

Individual disciplines and departments could engage their members in continuing professional growth: for instance, by forming disciplinary research teams and study groups, by sponsoring colloquia and debates. Across disciplines, theoretical issues are less sharply drawn, and norms of discourse inevitably somewhat looser. Still, faculty can come together in seminar settings, to teach one another, to reenter together the academic world as generalists. At the beginning, this may mean inviting "outside experts" to lead faculty in discussions, by way of norm setting. But community college faculty can relearn and rediscover together the excitement of intellectual exchange—precisely what nontraditional students perhaps most need to experience about academic life.

3. *Academic Cultural Audits.* Our earlier description of curricula as the expression of diverse educational agendas offered a view of the open-access college as the site of significant intellectual disagreement. Since our intellectual and educational traditions are multiple and diverse, there is nothing particularly bad about that. However, disagreement about the form and content of curricula and pedagogy cannot be institutionally productive when it remains hidden, unacknowledged, and undebated. The important first step toward strengthening the academic culture is identifying and surfacing the current mix of agendas. "Cultural audits" can be modeled on traditional curriculum audits, differing only in that they attempt to disclose the tacit dimensions of schooling: expectations, perceptions, symbols, practices.

Collegial staff development practices can help faculty to interpret their intellectual and pedagogical commitments, to see the diverse theoretical grounding of their eclectic educational practices. One approach we have found useful is for faculty in a workshop setting to examine formal classroom materials such as writing assignments and examination questions. Such materials are educational agendas in action—not what teachers say they are doing, or hope to be doing. They formally embody the intellectual demands of courses and classrooms—what students are really asked to do, what kinds of abilities are being cultivated and evaluated. The typology of educational agendas we developed earlier can be a useful model of a new vocabulary for describing the diverse conceptions of intellectual life presented in courses. But whether that is used or not, the important thing is to find ways for the classroom agendas to "go public" in a rigorous and challenging setting.

Confronting Disarticulation

Community colleges have never really come to terms with nontraditional student culture. Mostly, they haven't even noticed the cultural ensembles of students, and when they have they have interpreted them as collections of psychological traits. The ordinary ways of talking about students can be traced to that transposition. Students are unprepared for college, teachers may say; they lack skills and motivation. Perhaps, counselors may say, they lack self-esteem, or the concerns and pressures of their personal lives have to be dealt with before they can concentrate on their studies. What is needed, say teachers, is higher standards, more rigor. What is needed, say counselors, is "nurturing," a pedagogy of personal growth. The way that conversation usually ends is with somebody saying that we really need both: challenge in a nurturing setting, for instance.

Within canonical educational theory, student needs can be divided into the cognitive and the affective: the former the province of the classroom instructor, the latter residing with the counseling staff. This has resulted in a long-standing, barely muted conflict between the student service and academic staffs of open-access colleges. Teachers and counselors implicitly stand against one another, often conceiving, sometimes publicly avowing themselves to be protecting students against the other. Counselors explicitly define themselves as advocates for students in confrontations with teachers. Teaching faculty endure the expanded presence of counseling services in the hope that they may somehow reshape the mysterious student attitudes and behaviors that are so exasperating to teachers. But they remain deeply suspicious of the dominant social service ethos and therapeutic orientation of counselors. On both sides of the house, the exclusive concern with individual students obscures the cultural dynamics of nontraditionality. Nontraditional students create and reinforce in one another styles of thought and patterns of behavior—assumptions about school, society, and themselves.

When teachers think about changing students, they imagine acting on them one by one. And, given the highly anecdotal tilt of a practitioners' culture, teachers think they pretty much understand their students. Faculty routinely accept the standard distinction between the cognitive and the affective, and explain student failure as either a lack of skills or lack of motivation. Almost always they model student behavior as a breakdown of rational calculation: if students could only be brought to see where their interests truly lie, then they would begin to act more in line with teacher expectations, to turn their papers in on time, for instance. Teachers see their challenge as successfully structuring student experience so that rewards and punishments follow desired and undesired behavior respectively. The problem with this is that we all know too much about the students to have much confidence in that game. Students profess great interest in grades, and in pleasing teachers, but that doesn't seem to have much impact on how they act in class. As a group, either they do not run cost/benefit analyses of the sort imagined by teachers, or their analyses are systematically infected by considerations teachers do not anticipate; or else, whatever their calculations, their behaviors stick anyway, resisting their acts of will. Similarly, traditional classrooms presume teacherly authority; whether nontraditional students interpret that authority merely as illegitimate social power may perhaps be taken as an open question.

The point is not that teachers are either right or wrong in modeling individual student psychology in the standard ways. Rather, colleges and faculties should resist the temptation to think that they already understand their students, and that the problem is that students just don't understand them. Incomprehension is mutual.

1. *Student Culture Audits.* Almost all community colleges test the skill level of students at entrance and exit. We suggest that they conduct cultural audits of their student population as well. Student culture may vary quite dramatically from place to place, as neighborhood or ethnic cultures do. Colleges cannot rely on grand psychological theories or national studies; they have to assess the precise contours of the student culture at their own institutions.

The account of nontraditionality we have proposed can only be a kind of pointer since it has been almost entirely by contrast with traditional students. Nontraditional students, we said, are not like them in this way and that. But, once that has been recognized, the critical problem for institutions is discovering precisely what their students actually are like. What cultural styles, ways of acting and thinking, do they come with? How do they interpret their collegiate experience? Does their understanding of education and its relation to their lives change through their experience of college, or is it reinforced there?

Obviously these are large and difficult questions which colleges have not yet been prepared to investigate routinely and systematically. But, given the educational problem presented by a large nontraditional student population, open-access colleges ought to supplement their standard quantitative research with qualitative, ethnographic studies designed to discover how and where communications between college and students fire and mis-fire—things transcript analyses and forced-choice questionnaires can not reveal.

A full ethnographic examination of student culture would necessarily be a multilayered effort. One relatively easy part might consist of semistructured interviews and student focus group discussions led by appropriately trained faculty or other researchers. A student group identified at admission could be tracked and re-interviewed at intervals. Somewhat more ambitious, but likewise more rewarding, would be ethnographic studies targeted at understanding specific aspects of the college culture. To take one example, suppose ethnographers were to study a college's learning center. For them the big issues would be things like how education is portrayed and influenced through the normal processes and exchanges in the center—how students actually use the resources, for instance, or how peer tutors influence how other students think about courses and teachers.

2. *Building a Reflective Student Culture.* If colleges are to construct activities that can successfully initiate nontraditional students into academic culture, then faculty and administrators will have to be very attentive to the results of student culture audits. Otherwise, the danger is that colleges will continue to construct, and reconstruct, activities that are unintelligible to students, or that students will reinterpret in unfortunate and counterproductive ways. The results of student culture audits can be fed directly back into the curriculum through activities designed to help students understand their own academic styles and behaviors, and to see them as optional. Group rather than individual approaches are much more suited to accomplishing this.

One approach is to create settings which encourage students and faculty to discuss and interpret how students think and talk about education, about careers, about what resources are available therapy, since it aims to help students become more reflective about their ordinary, accustomed ways of conceiving those issues, and more open to alternatives. Although this strikes people initially as a counseling function, it actually is better located among the teaching faculty, since at the center of the conversation are large theoretical concerns: vocabularies, patterns of reasoning,

and modes of discourse. There is little to be gained by just telling
students some version of "this is how you should be thinking about
education, or about life." More movement can be gotten by encouraging reflection about those matters as a rigorous academic activity, by holding mirrors up to the student culture, by expanding
options available to students by enlarging their repertoire for conceiving their options.

Reordering the Curriculum

If the faculty professional culture is not strengthened, nor
the student culture appreciated, open-access colleges will be able
to make little headway on effective reform. But those are necessary and not sufficient conditions. The cultural exchange between
faculty and students happens through curriculum and pedagogy.
As things now stand, however, that communication is confused
and disordered.

The community college's ideological emphasis on creative
pedagogy has had unanticipated consequences. Although it has
freed faculty to concentrate on the classroom, it has also progressively isolated those classrooms, detached them from the very disciplines they are intended to represent. Individual teachers,
departments, and divisions have only loose intellectual responsibilities to each other, indeed, to anybody. Isolated intellectually, as
well as socially and institutionally, they lose sight of the overall
shape of students' collegiate experience, and how their own contribution fits in, or doesn't.

Now, as students move from course to course they encounter
a bewildering array of educational agendas which vie for their attention and their commitment. Even within individual courses,
competing practices associated with incommensurable notions of
rationality and of education send mixed and confusing signals to
students about the nature of their educational enterprise. We do
not wish necessarily to argue that any one particular educational
agenda is the best. Given the convoluted history that we sketched
earlier, it would be perfectly pointless to try to impose some one
agenda anyway, to try to get all teachers to do the same thing, to
have one educational tradition trump all the others. The curricular problem is not that teachers are doing the wrong things, but
that the mix of things is unacknowledged, uncoordinated, and consequently unintelligible to students.

Of course, students encounter teachers one by one, but the effect of any one or two naturally is limited. What really counts in their academic training is the corporate or community voice of the professoriate which presents an image of academic, intellectual, and professional life for students, models it for them and initiates them into it. However, that unity of purpose currently does not exist. What appears to faculty apologists to be an energizing harmony of diversity, may sound to students as a wild cacophony, a confusion of voices with no central chord.

A curriculum reform process which aims to clarify the confused communication between faculty and students would depend on administrators and faculty collegially agreeing about the proper mix of the various educational agendas, and how they would be formally represented in the curriculum. That aside, since regions, communities, students, and faculties are different, we do not think any single substantive curriculum proposal will make sense everywhere. But the big issues must be joined everywhere.

1. Reconceiving Introductory Courses. With few exceptions, disciplines are much weaker at community colleges than at universities where their position is preeminent. The gradual creep toward dilute generic and interdisciplinary frameworks for curricula suggests a tacit widespread suspicion that disciplines ought not be the basis on which curricula are organized for nontraditional students. We believe that to be much too strong, but that disciplines certainly have to be strengthened if they are to meaningfully shape students' collegiate experience.

For students at community colleges, introductory courses are their only experience of most disciplines. But what counts as an appropriate "introduction" to a discipline is a much more complicated question for community colleges than for the universities where such courses originated. At the university their functions are clear, if multiple. For some students introductory courses begin them on the trail to the major; for others they serve as part of their general education. Neither of these familiar functions is much of a guide to what courses should be like at community colleges.

If introductory courses in the disciplines are to contribute to the initiation of students into an academic culture, then disciplinary methods, norms, and practices have to form their cognitive core. Obviously, disciplines have certain commitments about information, but disciplines are not just aggregates of background information. Introductory courses that hide the theoretical perspectives and methodological commitments that constitute disciplines accelerate the curricular spin toward pale "generic" intellectual practices. For nontraditional students especially, introductory courses ought to disclose the nature of disciplines and engage them, if only in a preliminary way, in its practices.

2. *Decentralized Writing Instruction.* Writing Across the Curriculum programs are currently the only self-conscious efforts to affect the academic norms of discourse. Unfortunately, because WAC programs almost always emanate from English or composition departments, they most typically carry the mix of agendas developed there. Consequently, programs on that "centralized" model hold little hope for strengthening other disciplinary classrooms. Although there are historical reasons why the English department has been seen, on alternate days, as either the locus of the solution or the locus of the problem, no single department has the capacity, or the wisdom, to counter the academic drift. Neither the problem nor the solution is in the English department anymore than anywhere else. A collegiate solution is needed to the collegiate problem.

Academic cultural audits would include investigation of what disciplines do with language—with reading and writing, arguing, conversing, and understanding. As educational agendas tend to be mixed, so also we would expect writing conceptions to be—as a reflection of the uncertainty about the relation between language and thought that pervades composition classrooms. In some classrooms good writing may be just a matter of spelling or punctuation skills; elsewhere expressivist teachers may represent thought as a private ruminatory activity. And so on. Although obviously some of the writing agendas make much more sense for college students than others, the important point is that if writing, and thinking, are to really count in students' educations, then the agendas and pedagogical practices of the faculty have to be roughly congruent. For most disciplines, language is not introspective, nor skills nor abstract principles to be mastered. More characteristically, it is the medium of dialogue and debate, of the rough and tumble of minds in process.

In many ways, disciplinary faculty are better situated than composition teachers to affect students' language practices. For students, reading and writing and thought most meaningfully occur within particular academic situations. Unless those are bitted back toward triviality, they call on students to find their way into styles of thought, methods, and debates—conversations—that constitute the culture of the disciplines. If community colleges are to be academically strong, more importantly, if they are to offer students the chance to be academically competent, the disciplines cannot give up their methods and concerns, their rigor, in the name of generic skills. Although decentralized writing programs may take many forms, their common precondition is the agreement of disciplinary faculty, and of faculty across disciplines, about which education agendas will be represented within the curriculum, and what set of sustained practices constitute the academic culture.

CHAPTER 2

1. We recognize that these are becoming harder to find. One of the consequences of the massive expansion of higher education is that only the most elite colleges and universities have been insulated from the influx of nontraditional students, and they not entirely. Faculty at many middle level universities share the community college experience of trying to recall what traditional education looked like.

CHAPTER 3

1. For discussion of Taylorism see David Montgomery, *The Fall of the House of Labor* (1988); Harry Braverman, *Labor and Monopoly Capital* (1974); Thomas Hughes, *American Genesis* (1989).

2. On the influence of psychology on curriculum theory see Arthur Powell, *The Uncertain Profession* (1980), and Thomas S. Popkewitz, ed., *The Formation of School Subjects* (1989).

3. Although Hirsch's "cultural literacy" is most commonly identified with simple information acquisition, a reputation well-earned by long lists of essential cultural references, he is careful to offer a conservative version of critical literacy as well. Roughly, the idea is that students should be taught "schema" of thought, which turn out to be familiar inference patterns that allegedly command assent as "laws of thought."

4. As we will sketch in more detail later, since the cultural position of the humanities has become so confused and uncertain, those disciplines, much more than any other academic area, consists of a brew of mixed vocabularies, commitments, and practices drawn eclectically from several agendas.

5. For an excellent sketch of the relation between the Enlightenment and Romanticism see Charles Taylor's *Hegel* (1975), especially chapters 1 and 2.

6. The general movement described as "post foundational" includes thinkers as diverse as Rorty, Gadamer, Kuhn, Geertz, Polyani, Derrida, and Foucault. Despite very important differences, that rather impressive list is unified by a common rejection of the empiricist/positivist account of knowledge, of representational theories of "truth," of referential accounts of meaning and language, and of alogrithmic and mechanical reliance on "method." The overall tendency among them is toward the contextualizing, historicizing, and localizing of knowledge and method.

CHAPTER 4

1. In obvious ways the latter is a far more problematic affair. It raises immediately the question of the perspective from which commonality is to be construed, the theories that will supply the descriptive vocabulary, the canons of methodological rigor, and so on.

2. Remember that the issue here is not so much whether faculty at universities will agree that their students are advantaged in the ways described. As we argued in chapter one, only the most elite colleges any longer have many students with the kind of traditional academic preparation which once was the norm. Nevertheless, the idealization has a point, since it provides the model against which colleges measure themselves and their students. Almost all institutions suffer some effects of disarticulation; open-access colleges are just the farthest down that road. See for instance Michael Moffatt, *Coming of Age in New Jersey* (1989), a study of a flagship state university, which finds many of the symptoms of disarticulation that we describe.

CHAPTER 5

1. Many composition teachers argue the futility of detaching reading and writing from so-called content courses and recent movements have been directed at their reintegration. However, that has affected learning centers hardly at all. Correct writing concerns are left primarily with expert grammarians while advocates of "integration" couch their analyses of the role of writing in terms of clear writing: logic, organization, and, of course, clarity. At present, the most common form taken by the push to integrate clear writing principles with the various disciplines is the administrative device of "linked courses."

2. On the origins of the Romantically conceived self see Isaiah Berlin's *Against the Current: Essays in the History of Ideas* (1980), and

Charles Taylor's *Hegel* (1975). For recent studies of Romanticism see Cynthia Chase, *Decomposing Figures: Rhetorical Readings in the Romantic Tradition* (1986) and Charles J. Rzepka, *The Self as Mind: Vision and Identity in Wordsworth, Coleridge and Keats* (1986).

CHAPTER 6

1. Published materials for or about community college writing across the curriculum programs are quite sparse. So rather than citing textbooks designed for use at four-year colleges or universities, we have chosen to look carefully, and in detail, at how WAC practices and understandings are presented in *The Shortest Distance to Learning*. Given the sort of vanguard effort it was intended to be, especially as a collaboration between a major university and a large community college district, it is more than usually informative.

CHAPTER 7

1. Teachers returning to graduate school for further training may not be strengthening their disciplinary abilities at all. Many are "retooling" for teaching reading or writing to remedial students. Others pursue advanced degrees in education rather than their home disciplines. And, of course, there are now graduate programs specifically designed for community college teachers that are analogous to "teacher training" for elementary or high school.

2. Research on oral cultures has been almost completely concerned with preliterate cultures—archaic Greece, for instance—where it can be seen in pure form. But it would be a mistake to think of orality as something we've all left behind. Literate modes are not "wired into" the brain, nor even into societies. Both "literacy" and "orality" are not so much features or an individual person's brain, or consciousness, or cognitive structures, as they are particular social forms of cognitive organization; they are social performances.

3. North's description of practitioners' culture, on which we have drawn so heavily, is offered by him as a sketch of composition departments. We have expanded the range here to cover the community college faculty more generally, but, of course it is not irrelevant that those are so much dominated by composition teachers.

4. The frequent recent calls for teacher-conducted classroom research might be seen as making a virtue of necessity within a practitioners' culture (Goswami and Stillman, 1987; Cross, 1988). Although faculty may

not have the resources to talk and reflect as a collegial body, at least
"lore" can be strengthened by improving the ability of individual teachers
to interpret their experience. Quite in consonance with the primarily social organization of faculties, advocates of "classroom research" urge that
"teachers can serve each other as resources and consultants, sharing insights, observations and speculations" (Atwell, 1987:91).

American Association of Community and Junior Colleges. "Follow-up and Transfer of Two-Year College Students." Washington, D.C.: American Association of Community and Junior Colleges, 1979.

————. *The Future of Humanities Education at Community, Technical and Junior Colleges.* Washington, D.C.: American Association of Community and Junior Colleges, 1986.

Atwell, Nancie. "Class-Based Writing Research." In *Reclaiming the Classroom: Teacher Research as an Agency for Change,* Dixie Goswami and Peter R. Stillman, eds. New Jersey: Boynton/Cook, 1987.

Austin, J. L. *Sense and Sensibilia.,* ed. J. Geoffrey. New York: Oxford University Press, 1964.

Bartholomae, David. "Inventing the University." In *When A Writer Can't Write,* Mike Rose, ed. New York: Guilford, 1985.

Bazerman, Charles. "What Written Knowledge Does: Three Examples of Academic Discourse." *Philosophy of the Social Sciences* 11 (1981): 361–387.

Bellah, Robert N., Madsen, Richard, Sullivan, William M., Swidler, Ann, and Tipton, Steven M. *Habits of the Heart.* Berkeley and Los Angeles: University of California, 1985.

Bennett, William J. *To Reclaim a Legacy: A Report on the Humanities in Higher Education. Washington, D.C.:* National Endowment for the Humanities, 1984.

Benson, J. Kenneth, ed. *Organizational Analysis: Critique and Innovation.* Beverly Hills and London: Sage, 1977.

Berger, Peter L. *Invitation to Sociology.* New York: Doubleday, 1963.

Berlin, Isaiah. *Against the Current: Essays in the History of Ideas.* New York: Penguin, 1980.

Berlin, James A. "Contemporay Composition: The Major Pedagogical Theories." *College English* 44 (December 1982): 765–777.

————. *Rhetoric and Reality: Writing Instruction in American Colleges, 1900–1985* Carbondale: Southern Illinois University Press, 1987.

————. "Rhetoric and Ideology in the Writing Class." *College English* 50 (Sept. 1988): 477–494.

Bernstein, Alison R. "Urban Community Colleges and a Collegiate Education: Restoring the Connection." In *Colleges of Choice,* Judith S. Eaton, ed. New York: Macmillan, 1988.

171

Bizzell, Patricia. "Cognition, Convention and Certainty: What We Need to Know About Writing." *Pre/Text* 3 (1982): 213–243.

Blair, Catherine P. "Only One of the Voices: Dialogic WAC." *College English* 4 (April 1988): 383–389.

Bloom, Allan. *The Closing of the American Mind*. New York: Simon & Schuster, 1987.

Bobbitt, Franklin. "The Supervision of City Schools." In *Twelfth Yearbook of the National Society for the Study of Education*. Part I Bloomington, Illinois, National Society for the Study of Education, 1913.

———. *The Curriculum*. Boston: Houghton Mifflin, 1918.

———. *How To Make A Curriculum*. Boston: Houghton Mifflin, 1924.

Bolman, L. G. and Deal, T. E. *Modern Approaches to Understanding and Managing Organizations*. San Francisco: Jossey-Bass, 1984.

Boyer, Ernest and Levine, Arthur. *The Quest for a Common Learning*. Washington, D.C.: Carnegie, 1981.

Braverman, Harry. *Labor and Monopoly Capital; The Degradation of Work in the Twentieth Century*. New York: Monthly Review, 1974.

Brint, Steven and Karabel, Jerome. *The Diverted Dream: Community Colleges and the Promise of Educational Opportunity in America, 1900–1985*. New York: Oxford University Press, 1989.

Bruffee, Kenneth A. "Liberal Education and the Social Justification of Belief." *Liberal Education* 68 (1982): 95–113.

Bruffee, Kenneth A. "Collaborative Learning and the 'Conversation of Mankind.'" *College English* 46 (1984): 635–652.

———. "Social Construction, Language and the Authority of Knowledge: A Bibliographical Essay." *College English* 48 (December 1986): 773–790.

Buttenwieser, Peter L. "Achieving Fundamental Change Within in a Change-Resistant Environment: The Transfer Opportunities Program Experience in Community College of Philadelphia (1984–1987)." A report prepared for the Ford Foundation, August 1987.

Caldwell, Corrinne. "Implications of the One-Stage Career For Community College Faculty," *Ph.D. diss.*, University of Pennsylvania, 1985.

Callahan, Raymond. *Education and the Cult of Efficiency*. Chicago: University of Chicago Press, 1962.

Carnegie Foundation for the Advancement of Teaching. "Excerpts from the Prologue and Recommendations of 'Colleges: The Undergraduate Experience in America.'" *The Chronicle of Higher Education* 33 (10) 1986: 16.

Center for the Study of Community Colleges. *Transfer Education in American Community Colleges*. A Report to the Ford Foundation, 1985.

Charters, W. W. *Curriculum Construction*. New York: Macmillan, 1923.

Chase, Cynthia. *Decomposing Figures: Rhetorical Readings in the Romantic Tradition*. Baltimore: Johns Hopkins, 1986.

Chazen, M., ed. *Compensatory Education*. London: Butterworth, 1973.

Clark, Burton. "The 'Cooling Out' Function in Higher Education." *American Journal of Sociology* 65 (1960): 569–576.

——— . "The 'Cooling Out' Function Revisited." *In Questioning the Community College Role,* G. B. Vaughan, ed. *New Directions for Community Colleges* 32 (1980): 15–31.

Clowes, Donald A. "More Than a Definitional Problem." *Current Issues in Higher Education* 1 (1982): 1–12.

Cohen, Arthur M. *Dateline '79: Heretical Concepts for the Community College.* Beverly Hills: Glencoe Press, 1969.

Cohen, Arthur M. and Brawer, Florence B. *The American Community College.* San Francisco: Jossey-Bass, 1982.

——— . *The Collegiate Function of Community Colleges.* San Francisco and London: Jossey-Bass, 1987.

Coles, William E., Jr. *The Plural I: The Teaching of Writing.* New York: Holt, Rinehart and Winston, 1978.

——— . *Teaching Composing.* Rochelle Park, N.J.: Hayden, 1987.

Cross, K. Patricia. *Beyond the Open Door: New Students to Higher Education.* San Francisco: Jossey-Bass, 1971.

——— . *Accent on Learning: Improving Instruction and Reshaping the Curriculum.* San Francisco: Jossey-Bass, 1976.

Deal, Terrence E. and Kennedy, Allen A. *Corporate Cultures.* Reading, Mass.: Addison-Wesley, 1982.

Dorst, Walter H. and Sneeden, David. *Education for Social Efficiency.* Madison: University of Wisconsin Press, 1967.

Donovan, Richard A., Schaier-Peleg, Barbara, and Forer, Bruce. *Transfer: Making it Work.* Washington, D.C.: American Association of Community and Junior Colleges, 1987.

Dougherty, Kevin J. "The Politics of Community College Expansion: Beyond the Functionalist and Class-Reproduction Explanations." *American Journal of Education* 42 (May 1988): 351–393.

Dreeben, Robert. *On What is Learned in School.* Reading, Mass.: Addison-Wesley, 1968.

Eells, Walter C. *The Junior College.* Boston: Houghton Mifflin, 1931.

Eisner, Elliott W. *The Educational Imagination: On the Design and Evaluation of School Programs.* New York: Macmillan, 1979.

Elbow, Peter. *Writing Without Teachers.* New York: Oxford University, 1973.

Eliot, Charles. *Educational Reform: Essays and Addresses.* New York: Century, 1898.

——— . "A Turning Point in Higher Education." In *Handbook on Undergraduate Education,* Arthur Levine, ed. San Francisco: Jossey-Bass, 1978.

Emig, Janet. *The Composing Process of Twelfth Graders.* Research Report no. 13. Urbana: National Council of Teachers of English, 1971.

——— . "Writing as a Mode of Learning." *College Composition and Communication* 28 (1977): 105–129.

Faigley, Lester. "Competing Theories of Process: A Critique and a Proposal." *College English* 48 (October 1986): 527–540.

Fish, Stanley. *Is There a Text in this Class?: The Authority of Interpretative Communities.* Cambridge: Harvard University Press, 1980.

Foster, William. *Paradigms and Promises: New Approaches to Educational Administration.* Buffalo: Prometheus Books, 1986.

Fulwiler, Toby. "How Well Does Writing Across the Curriculum Work?" *College English* 46 (February 1984): 113–125.

———. "Evaluating Writing Across the Curriculum." In *Strengthening Programs for Writing Across the Curriculum,* Susan H. McLeod, ed. *New Directions for Teaching and Learning* 36 (Winter, 1988): 61–76.

Geertz, Clifford, *The Interpretation of Cultures.* New York: Basic Books, 1973.

———. *Local Knowledge.* New York: Basic Books, 1983.

Georgiou, Petro. "The Goal Paradigm and Notes Toward a Counter Paradigm." *Administrative Science Quarterly* 18 (1973): 291–310.

Goswami, Dixie and Stillman, Peter R., eds. *Reclaiming the Classroom: Teacher Research as an Agency for Change.* New Jersey: Boynton/Cook, 1987.

Gradori, Anna. *Perspectives on Organizational Theory.* Cambridge, Mass.: Ballinger, 1987.

Haskell, Thomas L., ed. *The Authority of Experts.* Bloomington: Indiana University Press, 1984.

Herrington, Anne J. "Writing to Learn: Writing Across the Disciplines." *College English* 43 (April 1981): 379–387.

———. "Classrooms as Forums for Reasoning and Writing." *College Composition and Communication* 36 (December 1985): 404–413.

Hirsch, E. D. *Cultural Literacy: What Every American Needs to Know.* Boston: Houghton Mifflin, 1987.

Horowitz, Helen L. *Campus Life: Undergraduate Cultures from the End of the Eighteenth Century to the Present.* Chicago: University of Chicago Press, 1987.

Hughes, Thomas P. *American Genesis: A Century of Invention and Technological Enthusiasm.* New York: Viking, 1989.

Jackson, Philip. *Life in Classrooms.* New York: Holt, Rinehart, 1968.

Jencks, Christopher and Riesman, David. *The Academic Revolution.* New York: Doubleday, 1968.

Karabel, Jerome. "Community Colleges and Social Stratification: Submerged Class Conflict in American Higher Education." *Harvard Educational Review* 42 (1972): 521–562.

Kimball, Bruce A. *Orators and Philosophers: A History of the Idea of Liberal Education.* New York: Teachers College Press, 1986.

Kinneavy, James L. *A Theory of Discourse.* New York: Norton, 1980.

Kintzer, Frederick C., ed. *Improving Articulation and Transfer Relationships. New Directions for Community Colleges* No. 39 (Sept. 1982).

Kintzer, Frederick C. and Wattenbarger, J. L. *The Articulation/Transfer Phenomenon: Patterns and Directions.* Washington, D.C.: American Association of Community and Junior Colleges, 1985.

Knoell, Dorothy M. and Medsker, Leland L. *From Junior to Senior College.* Washington, D.C.: American Council on Education, 1965.

Kozol, Jonathan. *Illiterate America.* New York: Anchor Press, 1985.

Krug, E. *The Shaping of the American High School, 1920–1941.* Madison: University of Wisconsin Press, 1972.

Kuh, George D. and Whitt, Elizabeth J. *The Invisible Tapestry: Culture in American Colleges and Universities.* ASHE-ERIC Higher Education Report No. 1 Washington, D.C.: Association for the Study of Higher Education, 1988.

Kuhn, Thomas. *The Structure of Scientific Revolutions.* 2nd ed. Chicago: University of Chicago Press, 1970.

Lieberman, Ann, ed. *Building a Professional Culture in Schools.* New York: Teacher's College, 1988.

Little, J. W. "Norms of Collegiality and Experimentation: Workplace Conditions of School Success." *American Educational Research Journal* 19 (1982): 325–340.

Lombardi, John. "The Decline of Transfer Education." Eric Clearinghouse, Topical Paper No. 70 (December 1979).

London, Howard. *The Culture of a Community College.* New York: Praeger, 1978.

———. "In Between: The Community College Teacher." *Annals of the American Academy of Political and Social Science,* vol. 448 (1980).

MacIntyre, Alasdair. *After Virtue.* Notre Dame: University of Notre Dame Press, 1981.

Macrorie, Ken. *Uptaught.* Rochelle Park: Hayden, 1970.

McCabe, Robert H. "The Educational Program of the American Community College." In *Colleges of Choice,* Judith S. Eaton, ed. New York: Macmillan, 1988.

McGrath, Dennis and Spear, Martin B. "The Humanities and Remedial Education: Reflections on the San Francisco Conference." *Community College Humanities Review,* 8 (1987): 77–82.

McKeachie, Wilbert J. *Teaching Tips: A Guidebook for the Beginning College Teacher.* Seventh Edition. Lexington, Mass.: D. C. Heath, 1978.

McLeod, Susan and Shirley, Susan. "National Survey of Writing Across the Curriculum Programs." In *Strengthening Programs for Writing Across the Curriculum,* Susan McLeod and Susan Shirley, eds. *New Directions for Teaching and Learning* 36 (Winter, 1988): 103–130.

Maimon, Elaine P. "Writing Across the Curriculum: Past, Present and Future." In *New Directions for Teaching and Learning,* ed. C. W. Griffin (December 1982): 67–73.

———. "Collaborative Learning and Writing Across the Curriculum." *Writing Program Administrator* 9 (Spring 1986): 9–15.

Medsker, L. L. *The Junior College: Progress and Prospect.* New York: Mc-Graw Hill, 1960.

Miller, Gary E. *The Meaning of General Education: The Emergence of a Curriculum Paradigm.* New York: Teachers College Press, 1988.

Mingle, James R. *Focus on Minorities: Trends in Higher Education Participation and Success.* Washington, D.C.: Education Commission of the States, 1987.

Moffatt, Michael. *Coming of Age in New Jersey.* New Brunswick: Rutgers University Press, 1989.

Montgomery, David. *The Fall of the House of Labor.* New York: Oxford University Press, 1988.

Moore, William M. *Against the Odds.* San Francisco: Jossey-Bass, 1970.

———. *Community College Response to the High Risk Student.* Eric Clearinghouse Monograph, 1981.

Myers, Greg. "Texts as Knowledge Claims: The Social Construction of Two Biology Articles." *Social Studies of Science* 15 (1985): 595–610.

Nettles, Michael T., ed. *Toward Black Undergraduate Student Equality in American Higher Education.* Conn.: Greenwood Press, 1988.

North, Stephen M. *The Making of Knowledge in Composition.* New Jersey: Boynton/Cook, 1987.

Ong, Walter J. *Orality and Literacy: The Technologizing of the Word.* London and New York: Methuen, 1982.

Ouchi, William G. and Wilkins, A. L. "Organizational Cultures." *Annual Review of Sociology* 11 (1985) 457–483.

Parnell, Dale. *The Neglected Majority.* Washington, D.C.: Community College Press, 1985.

Perry, William. *Forms of Intellectual and Ethical Development in the College Years.* New York: Holt, Rinehart and Winston, 1970.

Peters, Thomas J. and Waterman, Robert H. *In Search of Excellence.* New York: Harper & Row, 1982.

Pincus, Fred L. "The False Promises of Community Colleges: Class Conflict and Vocational Education." *Harvard Educational Review* 50 (1980): 332–361.

Pondy, L. R., Frost, P. J. and Dandridge, T. C., eds. *Organizational Symbolism.* Greenwich, Conn.: JAI, 1983.

Popkewitz, Thomas S., ed. *The Formation of School Subjects.* Philadelphia and London: Falmer, 1989.

Powell, Arthur G. *The Uncertain Profession.* Cambridge, Mass.: Harvard University Press, 1980.

———. Farrar, Eleanor, and Cohen, David K. *The Shopping Mall High School.* Boston: Houghton Mifflin, 1985.

Powell, J. P. "Some Nineteenth Century Views on the University Curriculum." *History of Education Quarterly* 5 (1965): 102–115.

Proctor, Robert E. *Education's Great Amnesia: Reconsidering the Humanities From Petrarch to Freud.* Bloomington, Indiana: University of Indiana Press, 1988.

Rabinow, Paul and Sullivan, William M., ed. *Interpretive Social Science: A Reader.* Berkeley and Los Angeles: University of California Press, 1979.

Reither, James A. "Writing and Knowing: Toward Redefining the Writing Process." *College English* 47 (October 1985): 620–628.

Richardson, Richard C., Jr., Fisk, Elizabeth A., and Okum, Morris A. *Literacy in the Open-Access College.* San Francisco: Jossey-Bass, 1983.

Richardson, Richard C. and Bender, Louis. *Minority Access and Achievement in Higher Education.* San Francisco: Jossey-Bass, 1987.

Riesman, David. *On Higher Education.* San Francisco: Jossey-Bass, 1980.

Robarts, James R. "The Quest for a Science of Education in the Nineteenth Century." *History of Education Quarterly* 8 (1968): 431–446.

Rohman, D. Gordon and Wlecke, Albert O. *Pre-Writing: The Construction and Application of Models For Concept Formation in Writing.* East Lansing: Michigan State University Press, 1964.

Rorty, Richard. *Philosophy and the Mirror of Nature.* Princeton: Princeton University Press, 1979.

————. *The Consequences of Pragmatism.* Minneapolis: University of Minnesota Press, 1982.

————. *Contingency, Irony, and Solidarity.* New York: Oxford, 1988.

Roueche, John E. *Salvage, Redirection or Custody? Remedial Education in the Community College.* Washington, D.C.: American Association of Community and Junior Colleges, 1968.

Roueche, John E. and Snow, Jerry J. *Overcoming Learning Problems.* San Francisco: Jossey-Bass, 1977.

Roueche, John E. and Kirk, Wade R. *Catching Up: Remedial Education.* San Francisco: Jossey-Bass, 1973.

Rzepka, Charles J. *The Self as Mind: Vision and Identity in Wordsworth, Coleridge and Keats.* Cambridge, Mass.: Harvard University Press, 1986.

Saufley, Ronald, Cowan, Kathryn, and Blake, J. Herman. "The Struggles of Minority Students at Predominantly White Institutions." In *Teaching Minority Students,* James Cones, John Noonan and Denise Janha, eds. San Francisco: Jossey-Bass, 1983.

Schein, Edgar H. *Organizational Culture and Leadership.* San Francisco: Jossey-Bass, 1985.

Schwartz, Barry. *The Battle for Human Nature.* New York: Norton, 1986.

Seidman, Earl. *In the Words of the Faculty: Perspectives on Improving Teaching and Educational Quality in Community Colleges.* San Francisco: Jossey-Bass, 1985.

Sergiovanni, Thomas J. and Corbally, J. E., eds. *Leadership in Organizational Culture.* Urbana: University of Illinois Press, 1984.

Seymour, Evan. "How should reading courses be read?" Paper presented at Fall, 1989 Community College of Philadelphia English Department Workshops on Reading and Writing.

Shaughnessy, Mina. *Errors and Expectations*. New York: Oxford University Press, 1977.

Shor, Ira. *Critical Teaching and Everyday Life*. Boston: South End Press, 1980.

——— . *Culture Wars: School and Society in the Conservative Restoration 1969–1984*. London and New York: Routledge and Kegan Paul, 1986.

Simmons, Joan M., ed. *The Shortest Distance to Learning: A Guidebook to Writing Across the Curriculum*. Los Angeles: Los Angeles Community College District and UCLA, 1983.

Simon, Linda. *Good Writing*. New York: St. Martin's Press, 1988.

Sizer, Theodore R. *Horace's Compromise: The Dilemma of the American High School*. Boston: Houghton Mifflin, 1984.

Sledge, Linda Ching. "The Community College Scholar," *Community College Humanities Review*, 8 (1987): 61–66.

Smith, Louise Z. "Why English Departments Should 'House' WAC." *College English* 50 (April 1988): 390–395.

Sullivan, William M. "The Humanities in the Civic Conversation: John Dewey's Public Philosophy Reconsidered." Unpublished Manuscript, 1987.

Swidler, Ann. "Culture in Action: Symbols and Strategies." *American Sociological Review* 51 (April 1986): 273–286.

Taylor, Charles. *Hegel*. New York: Cambridge University Press, 1975.

Tierney, William G. "Organizational Culture in Higher Education." *Journal of Higher Education*. 59 (January/February 1988): 1–21.

Tinto, Vincent. *Leaving College: Rethinking the Causes and Cures of Student Attrition*. Chicago: University of Chicago Press, 1987.

——— . "Stages of Student Departure: Reflections on the Longitudinal Character of Student Leaving." *Journal of Higher Education* 56 (July/August 1988): 438–455.

Tyler, Ralph. *Basic Principles of Curriculum and Instruction*. Chicago: University of Chicago Press, 1950.

——— . "The Curriculum—Then and Now." In *Proceedings of the 1956 Invitational Conference on Testing Problems*. Princeton: Educational Testing Service, 1957.

Van Maanen, John and Barley, S. R. "Occupational Communities: Culture and Control in Organizations." In *Research in Organizational Behavior*, Barry M. Staw, ed. Greenwich, Conn.: JAI, 1984.

Veysey, Laurence. *The Emergence of the American University*. Chicago: University of Chicago Press, 1965.

Weddington, Doris. *Faculty Attitudes in Two Year Colleges*. Los Angeles: Center for the Study of Community Colleges, 1976.

Weick, Karl. "Administering Education in Loosely Coupled Schools." *Phi Delta Kappan* (June 1982): 673–686.

Weis, Lois. *Between Two Worlds: Black Students in an Urban Community College*. Boston: Routledge and Kegan Paul, 1985.

Wexler, Philip. *Social Analysis of Education: After The New Sociology.* London and New York: Routledge & Kegan Paul, 1987.

White, Hayden V. *Metahistory: The Historical Imagination in the Nineteenth Century.* Baltimore: Johns Hopkins Press, 1973.

Wilson, Reginald and Melandez, S. E. *Minorities in Higher Education: Third Annual Status Report.* Washington, D.C.: American Council on Education, 1984.

Young, Art and Fulwiler, Toby, eds. *Writing Across the Disciplines: Research into Practice.* New Jersey: Boynton/Cook, 1986.

Zwerling, L. Steven. *Second Best: The Crisis of the Community College.* New York: McGraw-Hill, 1976.

————, ed. *The Community College and Its Critics. New Directions for Community Colleges* 54 (June 1986).